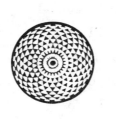

A STUDY GUIDE
COMMENTARY

A STUDY GUIDE
COMMENTARY

PHILIPPIANS

HOWARD F. VOS

ZONDERVAN
PUBLISHING HOUSE
OF THE ZONDERVAN CORPORATION
GRAND RAPIDS, MICHIGAN 49506

PHILIPPIANS: A STUDY GUIDE COMMENTARY

Copyright © 1975 by The Zondervan Corporation
Grand Rapids, Michigan

Library of Congress Catalog Card Number 74-25349

Fourth printing July 1980
ISBN 0-310-33863-8

Printed in the United States of America

Contents

A Beginning Word

We like to get mail. Often the question rings through a home, a summer camp, a school, or an office, "Did the mail come yet?" And often, especially at home, the response is, "Yes, there is a pile of stuff, but nothing important."

Letters have special significance in terms of who wrote them — a mother, father, fiancée, the President of the United States, God. Most New Testament letters were important to their recipients because they were from the apostle Paul who was their spiritual father. But more important, the recipients accepted them as inspired by the Holy Spirit and therefore from God. Thus they treated the contents of these letters as binding on them for life on earth and instructive for them of what to expect in the life to come.

One of the most beautiful of all Paul's letters is the one he sent to the church at Philippi, the first church founded in Europe. The apostle wrote to thank these friends for their gifts of money and for standing with him in other ways in the work of the gospel. But he also sought to deal with the problem of disunity that plagued them. Because the question of church union, factious struggles, and defective human relationships bother contemporary congregations of Christians, the Book of Philippians has a message as relevant for today as for the church that first received it.

More important, however, Philippians has much to say about God, the salvation He has provided through the work of Christ, man's fellowship with God, and growth in the spiritual life. In our day of relativism and rapid change, any document that can say something conclusive and abiding about relations with both God and other human beings has to be remarkable indeed, and certainly worth paying attention to. Here is a first-class letter. Postmark: heaven. Sender: God. Addressee: you.

CHAPTER 1

Founding of the Church at Philippi

Second missionary journey begins. The great council of Jerusalem was over (Acts 15:1-35). The mother church had taken its stand. Gentile Christians were not to be required to keep the law of Moses, and a record of the decision was sent to Antioch in the hands of Barnabas and Paul, Judas Barsabbas, and Silas. After delivering their message Paul and Barnabas stayed in Antioch for a while preaching and teaching. Then stirred with concern for the converts of the first missionary journey, they decided to travel to the interior of Asia Minor (modern Turkey) to visit them again (Acts 15:36). Barnabas wanted to take John Mark along, but Paul was opposed, so the two parted company. Barnabas took Mark to Cyprus and Paul chose Silas and set out for Asia Minor. Probably they began their journey in the early spring of A.D. 50.

This time Paul went overland. The road led north through the Syrian Gates and into the fertile plain of Cilicia. Passing through Tarsus, the main city of Cilicia and Paul's hometown, the missionary pair walked north through the Cilician Gates and ultimately reached the towns of Derbe, Lystra, Iconium, and Antioch of Pisidia. At Lystra Timothy joined the apostolic company.

Call to Macedonia. After the group ministered to believers in Antioch of Pisidia, they felt compelled to go on to tell the good news to others who had not yet heard the gospel. But the Holy Spirit made it clear to them that they should not preach in the Roman province of Asia, which occupied the western third of Asia Minor. So they went north into Mysia, but the Holy Spirit stopped them from preaching there also. Finally they came to the seaport of Troas, located about ten miles south of the western end of the Dardanelles (ancient Hellespont). There Paul had a vision in the night. In it a man from Macedonia appeared to him and begged him to come over into Macedonia and help them (Acts 16:9). Evidently this plea carried with it a recognition of the inadequacy of Greek culture, glorious though its heritage may have been, to meet the spiritual needs of mankind. It was also a request for Paul to come and give the Macedonians the gospel of Christ. Excited about what had happened, presumably Paul immediately told the others. Together they agreed that God was calling them to preach in Macedonia.

On to Philippi. Without delay they set sail across the northern Aegean. Following the practice of the times, they sailed during the day and dropped anchor at night at some port along the way. The first night they reached the island of Samothrace and on the second day came to Neapolis on the mainland of Macedonia. Luke had joined them earlier at Troas. Some argue that he was a native of Philippi.

Neapolis was beautifully situated on a promontory which stretched out into the bay. Apparently the missionaries had no plan to evangelize there because they turned inland along the much-traveled road to Philippi, some thirteen miles away (Acts 16:12). The road ascended the Symbolon Hills, which reach a height of 500 feet, and descended into the plain of Philippi. As they neared the city they moved onto the Egnatian Way, the main Roman road across Macedonia, which ran through the middle of Philippi.

Historical backgrounds. Philippi was more than 400 years old when Paul arrived. Philip II (father of Alexander the Great) had founded the city in 360 B.C., and in doing so replaced the old Thracian settlement of Crenides. The town was significant to Philip as the chief mining center in the Pangaeus gold fields (west of Philippi), which provided him with revenue for his gold currency, the support of his army, and the bribery of his enemies. While these important mines seem to have been largely exhausted by the time Macedonia passed into Roman hands, the Greek government is currently trying to discover new veins of ore in this region.

When Rome utterly defeated Macedonia at the battle of Pydna in 168 B.C., she divided the kingdom into four antonomous republics. Philippi was in the first (farthest east) of these. In 148 B.C. the entire territory became the Roman province of Macedonia. Philippi's lot was not a very happy one in subsequent years. The gold mines were worked out and the civil wars that followed the death of Julius Caesar brought great hardship. It will be remembered from Shakespeare's *Julius Caesar* or some other source that Brutus and Cassius committed suicide on the battlefield at Philippi in 42 B.C.

After this battle Roman veterans were settled on the site, which was renamed "Colonia Julia Philippensis" in honor of the victory of the cause of Julius Caesar (Acts 16:12). When Octavian (later Augustus Caesar) won the battle of Actium in 31 B.C. and became sole ruler of the empire, he designated the city as a colony for defeated supporters of Mark Antony evicted from Italy, and changed its name to "Colonia Augusta Julia Philippensis." As a colony Philippi enjoyed many political and economic privileges, including exemption from imperial taxes. Colonies were a little bit of Italy set down on foreign shores, and their government was patterned closely after that of the municipalities of Italy. As the Acts narrative suggests, inhabitants of such colonies were proud of their privileged position.

Church planting. Owing to the fact that Philippi was a military and agricultural rather than a commercial center, few Jews lived there when the missionary party arrived and they could find no synagogue in town. Had there been ten heads of Jewish families in Philippi, they would have been obligated to establish a synagogue. Paul and his companions discovered a little group of Jews holding a prayer meeting by a riverside. The fact that the group met outside the city probably indicates they were well beyond the pomerium or sacred boundary within which foreign deities were not permitted.

Here by the riverside, missions in Europe had their small beginnings. Lydia, a businesswoman from Thyatira in Asia Minor, a seller of purple cloth, was converted along with her household (Acts 16:14, 15). Apparently she was a Gentile who had become a Jewish proselyte or a god-fearer. Immediately she opened her guest rooms to the evangelists. Later, a demented slave girl who served her masters as something of a fortuneteller was restored to normalcy by the apostle. Her masters, upset over a loss of revenue, stirred up a riot against Paul. Charging that he was spreading teachings that would destroy the Philippians' Roman way of life, they dragged Paul and Silas into the agora or marketplace and accused the missionaries before the magistrates. These officials commanded that Paul and Silas be beaten and thrown into prison, ordering the jailer to keep them securely (Acts 16:22-24). What a discouraging state of affairs! Though Paul had received a vision of a *man* from Macedonia, the emphasis so far was on women. And the converts weren't even Macedonian. To top it all off, they found themselves beaten and in jail for having answered the call.

Undaunted by their sufferings, Paul and Silas prayed and sang in their cell. As they did so, an earthquake shook the prison to its very foundations and opened all the cell doors. Fearing that all his prisoners had escaped, and that he would suffer death for dereliction of duty, the jailer attempted to commit suicide. But Paul called out to him that all his charges were still there and he should have no fear of punishment. Undone by the whole chain of events, the jailer's heart was prepared for a profession of faith in Christ and he believed along with his household. Like Lydia, he showed Paul and Silas kindness and immediately treated their lacerated backs.

The next morning the city officials sent word to the prison to discharge the prisoners, but Paul decided to let them squirm a little. He responded that as Roman citizens he and Silas had rights before the law. A Roman should not be beaten until properly tried and sentenced by a court. Then he demanded that the magistrates come in person and release the missionary pair from jail. Thoroughly disturbed, the officials promptly did so and then asked them to leave town to avoid further trouble (Acts 16:36-39). Why the issue of citizenship had not come up the previous day is not clear. The niceties of rights do not always surface during a mob scene. And perhaps it did not occur to the town officials that these foreigners would have Roman citizenship, a privilege then enjoyed by a small minority of people in the Roman Empire.

After Paul and Silas had had a chance to rest and recuperate at the house of Lydia, and to encourage the fledgling church, they left on the Egnatian Way for Thessalonica. They left Luke behind, as is clear from the fact that the "we" phraseology, always used when Luke accompanied Paul, ceased abruptly. The narrative is described in the third person until Paul left Philippi on his last journey to Jerusalem, some five years later (Acts 20:6). If Luke remained at Philippi during the entire interim, some explanation is provided for the solid establishment of the church there and its peculiar interest in helping Paul over the years. This church more than any other is singled out for its gifts toward the apostle's support. They sent him at least four gifts (2 Cor. 8:3, 4; 11:8, 9; Phil. 4:10-14, 15, 16). It seems that Paul visited the city on his third missionary journey (Acts

19:22; 20:1) and again between his first and second imprison-
ments in Rome (1 Tim. 1:3).*

Archaeological rediscovery. Before going on to consider such
questions as the authorship, date, and purpose of writing this
epistle, some comments on the archaeology of Philippi are in
order. The French School at Athens worked at the site 1914-1938
and the Greek Archaeological Service has been active there since
World War II. While important beginnings have been made, much
is left to be done at Philippi. As usual, attention has focused on a
limited number of major structures in the center of town. The
agora, center of Greek life, where the mob scene and judgment of
Acts 16 took place, is a large rectangular area 300 feet long and
150 feet wide. On its northern side stood a rectangular podium
with steps leading up to it on either side. This apparently was
the place where magistrates dispensed justice. Although the agora
was much rebuilt during the reign of Marcus Aurelius in the
second century A.D., the general plan apparently is essentially the
same as it was in Paul's day. Along its north side ran the Egnatian
Way.

The success of the gospel at Philippi is evident from the fact
that imposing ruins of great churches may be seen. At the south
side of the agora stand remains of a sixth-century church known
as Basilica B. Just north of the agora, across the modern high-
way, lie ruins of a large fifth-century church known as Basilica
A. East of the agora in an area of recent excavation may be seen
remains of another fifth-century church flanked by a third-cen-
tury bath.

Excavators at Philippi have made other discoveries. Near
Basilica B stood a palestra or gymnastic center in the second century A.D. Adjacent to that is one of the best-preserved latrines
in the Roman Empire. In 1973 new excavations went forward at

*The writer holds that Paul was released from his first Roman im-
prisonment and made a fourth missionary journey. Three reasons will suf-
fice to support the point. 1) Eusebius of Caesarea in his early fourth-century
history said Paul was released from his first Roman imprisonment, resumed
his preaching tours, was imprisoned in Rome a second time and martyred
(*Ecclesiastical History,* 2.22). 2) Romans 15:24, 28 describe a prospective
trip to Spain, which various early church fathers say he made. Certainly he
did not make it before his first Roman imprisonment. 3) Philemon 22
and Philippians 1:25, 26; 2:23, 24 evidence a confidence on Paul's part
that he would be released from prison and would return to Philippi and
Colosse. A high view of inspiration would not regard these statements as
merely idle wishes of the author.

the east wall and gate of the city. Construction there has yet to be fully interpreted. Above the town towers the acropolis of Philippi, over 1000 feet high. On its eastern slope are well-preserved remains of a Greek theater, which was in its prime during Paul's visits there. Near the theater was a temple to Egyptian gods constructed early in the first century A.D. While much remains to be unearthed at Philippi, we are beginning to get some appreciation of the magnificence of the place during early Christian centuries when the gospel was first preached there.

Importance of Philippi to us. Philippi was not just any old place — an insignificant out-of-the-way Roman colony of the first century. It was the beachhead of Christianity in Europe. The establishment of the church there marks the intrusion of Christianity into the culture of the continent that would most influence world history down to the present. It is the continent from which most of our own cultural and religious heritage comes.

FOR FURTHER STUDY

1. Read the account of the founding of the church at Philippi in Acts 16 in three different English versions if possible.

2. Read articles in a Bible dictionary or Bible encyclopedia on Philippi and Philippians.

3. Locate Philippi on a map of Greece. Trace the route of Paul's second missionary journey.

4. Do you have any thoughts on why God sent a vision of a man from Macedonia instead of somewhere in North Africa — e.g., Alexandria?

CHAPTER 2

Background Issues

Authorship. Paul's authorship of the Book of Philippians is one of the most assured facts of biblical scholarship. The writer calls himself Paul in 1:1. Although he associates Timothy with him in the verse, he does not mean to imply coauthorship. This becomes clear from the fact that the writer plans to send Timothy to them (2:19), thus separating himself from Timothy, and that over fifty times in this short letter he refers to himself in the first person singular. The Pauline stamp is everywhere evident in Philippians; the simple, direct outpouring of the apostle's great heart could hardly be counterfeited.

What the book claims for itself in terms of authorship is supported by adequate testimony in the early church. Clement of Rome in the first century; Ignatius, Polycarp, and Irenaeus in the second century, and numerous church leaders thereafter gave witness to the existence of the book, its Pauline authorship, and its character as inspired Scripture. As early as about 140 the heretic Marcion included Philippians in his canon and about 175 the book appeared in the Muratorian Canon. It was of course recognized as one of the twenty-seven books of the New Testament canon at the Council of Chalcedon in 451. Today hardly a scholar of any note seriously questions either Paul's authorship or the integrity of the text of Philippians.

Place of writing. That Paul wrote this letter while in prison is evident from the text. In fact, Philippians is linked commonly with Ephesians, Colossians, and Philemon as a prison epistle. Where that imprisonment may have been is another question. Actually the issue has some rather technical aspects and deserves more extended attention than can be given to it here, but some brief comments are in order. Three places of imprisonment are suggested: Caesarea, Ephesus, and Rome.

That Paul was imprisoned in Caesarea in Palestine for about two years (as long as at Rome) is known (Acts 24:27), but the circumstances were different. Although his friends had access to him in both places, there is no indication he had the freedom to minister in Caesarea that he did in Rome. In Caesarea he was rather effectively confined but in Rome he maintained himself at his own expense under a kind of house arrest. The greater relaxation in the apostle's situation is reflected in all the prison epistles and it would seem therefore that they were written from Rome. Moreover, it is not likely that Onesimus, an escaped slave, would have made his way to Caesarea, a relatively small town, or that he would have had opportunity to minister to Paul on a prolonged basis there. In Rome he could have lost himself easily in the crowd of slaves and freedmen and could have enjoyed easy access to Paul. Furthermore, Paul did not have any real expectation of release from Caesarean imprisonment as he did from detention in Rome. If these epistles had been written in Caesarea, they would not have breathed the same degree of optimism that they do (e.g., Philem. 22; Phil. 1:25, 26).

Arguments for Ephesian imprisonment at the time Paul wrote Philippians or other Prison Epistles is based on such passages as 1 Corinthians 15:32; 2 Corinthians 1:8-10; 11:23. The first refers to fighting with wild beasts at Ephesus (presumably imprisonment would precede a fight in the arena), and speaks of his life being in danger every hour. The second alludes to a sentence of death on Paul in Asia (probably Ephesus), but God rescued him from the great danger. The third mentions being in prison frequently, but Acts records only one earlier imprisonment (at Philippi). Perhaps one of these was at Ephesus where hostility was fierce. Moreover, it is argued that the several journeys alluded to between the church at Philippi and Paul in prison would be possible if the shorter distance between Ephesus and Philippi were involved instead of the longer journey between Philippi and Rome. For instance, news of Paul's imprisonment had to reach Philippi, a gift had to be collected and sent with Epaphroditus, word of Epaphroditus' illness had to reach Philippi, and a report of the church's concern over his illness had to get back to Paul.

While these and several other more technical and involved suggestions make something of a case for Ephesian authorship, they are not conclusive. There was extensive contact between Rome and other parts of the Empire, and the movements just noted could have occurred between the capital and Philippi in a two-year period. Moreover, there is no real proof that Paul was imprisoned in Ephesus; if he was, there is no indication that it would have been a confinement of any duration. Reference to

Paul's fighting wild beasts at Ephesus usually is taken figuratively to indicate the ferocity of his opposition.

Rome still remains the most likely location of Paul's imprisonment when he wrote Philippians and the other Prison Epistles. We know that Paul was imprisoned there for two years (Acts 28:30), that he had a high degree of freedom to preach the gospel during that period of time, and that in the Roman church existed the kind of jealousy and opposition to Paul that could bring on the difficulties or affliction indicated in Philippians 1. While the Praetorium (Phil. 1:13; "palace" in KJV) can refer to members of the Praetorian Guard (elite troops of the Empire) on assignment in various parts of the Empire, such men would not likely be on assignment in Ephesus because Asia was a senatorial province and therefore under direct control of the Senate rather than the Emperor. Moreover, it is more natural to think of the Praetorian Guard as connected with Rome because the camp of the guard was located just outside the city limits. Although the reference to "Caesar's household" in Philippians 4:22 could apply to some of Caesar's representatives on assignment in Ephesus, it is likewise more natural to think of them as part of his staff in the city of Rome.

Date of writing. When Philippians was written cannot be stated with certainty. There are several views as to when the Roman imprisonment took place., Two of the best suggestions seem to be 59-61 and 60-62. The comings and goings between Philippi and Rome mentioned earlier seem to require that the book was written near the end of the imprisonment. Therefore composition probably took place in 61 or 62.

Reason for writing. Philippians often is spoken of as a thank you letter. The church at Philippi had sent Paul a gift and Epaphroditus, the bearer, who had contracted a serious illness in Rome, was now sufficiently recovered to return home (2:25-30). It was only natural that Paul would take the opportunity not only to thank the church for their gift and to speak a kind word for Epaphroditus, but also to deal with several other issues.

His friends at Philippi evidently were somewhat upset over his imprisonment and the opposition he encountered because he went to considerable effort to point out in chapter 1 that God was using the entire situation for His glory and the spread of the gospel. Paul's severe rebuke of Jewish legalism in chapter 3 would seem to indicate that some Judaizing propagandists were troubling this predominantly Gentile church or were threatening to do so. Throughout the epistle he deals with disunity and makes appeals for unity or harmony, in part because of some apparent problem in the Philippian church, and in part because of conflicts in the church at Rome which were plaguing him. Also, Paul tucked in some exhortations about living the Christian life: for example, steadfastness in the face of suffering (1:27-30) and an exemplary thought life (3:8).

Theme of the epistle. Even a quick survey of commentaries on Philippians reveals a considerable difference of opinion as to what the message of the book really is. Several have concluded that Christ is the theme of the book. This was the position of H. A. Ironside in his *Notes on Philippians.* He developed his discussion under the following headings: Christ, the Believer's Life; Christ, the Believer's Example; Christ, the Believer's Object; and Christ, the Believer's Strength. Similarly, Norman B. Harrison chose the title *His in Joyous Experience* and used as his chapter headings Christ — the Life of Life; Christ — the Pattern of Life; Christ — the Goal of Life; and Christ — the All-sufficiency of Life.

Following the fact that "joy" or "rejoice" appears sixteen times in the Greek text (1:4, 18, 25; 2:2, 17, 18, 28, 29; 3:1; 4:1, 4, 10), A. T. Robertson adopted as the title of his commentary *Paul's Joy in Christ.* Somewhat similar is John F. Walvoord's approach in *Philippians: Triumph in Christ.* He discusses triumph in suffering, in servce, in Christ, and in anxiety. Impressed with the emphasis on the gospel in the book (appears nine times), Merrill C. Tenney chose the title *Philippians: The Gospel at Work* for his study, and dealt with such topics as the beginning, fellowship, pattern, experience, and effects of the gospel. These examples, and many others that could be noted, underscore the fact that biblical books commonly have more than one theme and that one should not claim that his approach to the study of a book is the only way.

It seems there is yet another outstanding message in Philippians that has been commonly neglected in the literature — the subject of unity. Even a cursory reading of the epistle will turn up constant allusions to the theme. Several verses include the phrase "you all" or the word "all" and indicate that the apostle is emphasizing the fact he is speaking to the entire Philippian church and not several factions. Consider also other references to his desire for unity, as expressed in the words "one" or "same," and his command in 2:14, "Do all things without murmurings and disputings." A passage which, probably more than any other, expresses the thought of the entire epistle, and therefore serves as the key, is 2:1-5. There one finds the basis for unity — blessings of the Christian life; the exhortation to unity — "be of the same mind"; and the means of unity — humility and the consideration of the needs of others.

A further reading of the book with this central thought in mind will show how the theme of unity is developed throughout the book. Paul begins the epistle with a salutation "to all the saints in Christ Jesus which are in Philippi." This is a different approach from that employed in his other letters to churches, with the exception of Romans, where he also emphasizes "all." The reason for doing so in Romans, however, seems to be that the apostle desires to give a unity to the Roman Christian community which consists of churches meeting in a number of private homes (see Rom. 16).

The author then continues to emphasize the theme in making prayer for "you all" (Phil. 1:4); in believing that the Lord would keep "you all" unto the day of Christ (1:7); in declaring his concern for "you all" (1:8); in stating that it is needful for him to abide with "you all" (1:25); in exhorting them to stand fast in one spirit, striving for the faith of the gospel (1:27), and to live with singleness of purpose and love and without faction (2:2); his rejoicing is with "you all" (2:17); Epaphroditus shared Paul's concern for "you all" (2:26). A further emphasis on single-mindedness appears in 3:15, 16; and in 4:2 he exhorts two women who seem to be ringleaders in factional strife to put away their differences. In conjunction with the general theme of unity, two special problems arise. The first of these relates to Judaism and the Judaizers (3:1-11) and the second to Christian perfection (3:12-16).

Of course, the greatest passage in the whole book is 2:1-11. While it is a magnificent declaration concerning the person of Christ, it must be seen here in connection with the fact that all division will cease and harmony will be restored when men have the mind of Christ and live with such a humility of life that they do not infringe upon the rights of others. When such encroachment ceases on the part of all, unity will be restored. The following outline shows how this theme is developed in the book.

PHILIPPIANS: AN APPEAL FOR CHRISTIAN UNITY

Introduction (1:1-11)
  A. Salutation to all (1:1, 2)
  B. Thanksgiving and prayer for all (1:3-11)
  I. Paul's Imprisonment as Related to the Question of Unity (1:12-30)
      A. Toleration of disunity in motives for evangelistic work (1:12-18)
      B. Paul's preservation to promote a continuation of their growth in grace (1:19-26)
      C. Exhortation to unity while Paul remains in prison for a time (1:27-30)
 II. The Mind of Christ: The Source of All Unity (2:1-30)
      A. Nature: Humility of spirit (2:1-11)
          1. Exhortation to unity based on the mind of Christ (2:1-4)
          2. The mind of Christ in action: obedient even unto death (2:5-8)
          3. Exaltation by the Father (2:9-11)
      B. Product: Application of the mind of Christ (2:12-16)
      C. Examples: Those who possess the mind of Christ (2:17-30)
          1. Paul (2:17, 18)
          2. Timothy (2:19-24)
          3. Epaphroditus (2:25-30)
III. The Biographical Appeal for Unity: Answers from Paul's Experience to the Problems Causing Disunity (3:1-21)
      A. Paul's righteousness (3:1-16)
          1. Not of the law but of Christ (3:1-11)
          2. Not yet at stage of perfection (3:12-16)
      B. Paul's Example (3:17-21)
 IV. Exhortations That Will Lead to Unity (4:1-9)
      A. Plea for steadfastness (4:1)
      B. Settlement of differences between women in the church (4:2, 3)
      C. Rejoicing, prayer, and the resultant peace of God (4:4-7)
      D. Controlled thought life (4:8, 9)
  V. Thanksgiving for their Gift: A Representation of their United Action (4:10-20)

Conclusion: Greetings from All to All (4:21-23)
    A. Greetings (4:21, 22)
    B. Benediction (4:23)

FOR FURTHER STUDY

1. Read the sections on Philippians in D. E. Hiebert's *Introduction to the Pauline Epistles* and E. F. Harrison's *Introduction to the New Testament*.

2. Under "Authorship" the comment is made, "the simple, direct outpouring of the apostle's great heart could hardly be counterfeited." Find several examples of this outpouring in Philippians.

3. If you choose "joy" as the theme of Philippians, how would you outline the book?

4. If Philippians was written in A.D. 61, eleven years had elapsed since Paul first preached at Philippi. List in order the major events of his life during those years. Acts 16 to 28 will provide most of the information.

CHAPTER 3

Introduction

(Phil. 1:1-11)

As a result of archaeological and literary discoveries, we now know that Paul's letters follow the same general pattern as the secular letters of his time. Whether for personal or business purposes, letters of that day commonly began with the name of the writer and continued with the name of the reader and a greeting. Then came the body of the letter, followed by greetings and farewell. The chief difference in the form of Paul's letters is that he normally added thanksgiving for the readers after the greeting. And of course the content was completely different in tone. He used a spiritual greeting (grace and peace) instead of a secular term, and his purpose for writing was always to further the kingdom of God.

A. SALUTATION TO ALL (1:1, 2)

The writer and his associate. The writer simply calls himself Paul, not Paul the apostle, as he frequently does elsewhere. This is a personal, informal letter to a beloved church in which there was no real challenge to his authority or his message (as in 2 Corinthians or Galatians), nor is this an authoritative exposition of Christian doctrine (as in Romans).

Paul associates Timothy with him in the address because of his close ties with them. Timothy assisted Paul in establishing the church at Philippi (Acts 16:1, 13; 17:14) and had visited them at least twice since (Acts 19:22; 20:3, 4). Now Paul is preparing to send Timothy to them again (Phil. 2:19-23). He likewise joined Timothy's name with his in the two Thessalonian epistles and 2 Corinthians. Some have thought that Paul mentioned Timothy here because he served as Paul's secretary, taking the letter by dictation, but there is no hint in Philippians that Paul used a scribe. Apparently he wrote it with his own hand.

Certainly Paul did not mean to imply that Timothy was co-author of the letter. Beginning in verse 3 he writes in the first person singular and maintains that approach throughout the letter. In 2:19 he refers to Timothy in the third person, definitely distinguishing himself from Timothy as the writer.

Paul identifies himself and Timothy as "servants of Jesus Christ." In the Greek the word is *doulos,* "bondservant" or "slave." However, Paul evidently does not mean to imply that he is an abject slave of Christ, chafing at the bit and longing for freedom. His true attitude comes out in 1 Corinthians 7:22, where he describes himself as a bondservant, but the Lord's freeman, free in Christ. Put in the larger context of Paul's teaching about salvation, the Corinthians reference would remind us that the unsaved person is enslaved to sin and condemned under the penalty of judgment. Christ has redeemed the believer by His work on the cross and set him free from the condemnation of sin. And through the indwelling ministry of the Holy Spirit God has given him a new power to resist Satan and evil of all sorts, and thus a new freedom from the controlling power of sin.

But Paul does not view the believer as free to do whatever he wants. Having been bought by Christ, the individual now belongs to Him and has the responsibility to glorify God in his mind and body (1 Cor. 3:23; 6:19, 20). If one is owned by Christ, that means his body, his mind, his time, his talents, and material assets all belong to Christ. He belongs to another and owns nothing. He is simply a steward and must spend time, talents, and money at Christ's direction (1 Cor. 4:1; 1 Peter 4:10).

Addressees. Paul and Timothy, bondslaves of Jesus Christ, address themselves to all the saints in Christ Jesus at Philippi. The address is to all individual Christians. The saints (holy ones) are individuals set apart (basic meaning of "holy") or consecrated to God's purposes. This certainly is not a new thought. Again and again in the Old Testament God's people, the Israelites, were spoken of as holy or set apart to God (e.g., Exod. 19:6; Deut. 7:6; 14:2, 21, etc.). Now Christians likewise have this special relationship to God and have become a "holy nation" (1 Peter 2:9). So Paul and Timothy, bondservants, send greetings to those who themselves are set apart for God's purposes and likewise belong to Him in a special way.

Certainly this reference to holiness does not imply actual holiness but holiness as a proper characteristic of those calling themselves believers in Philippi. Positionally they were set apart for God's purposes when they believed and progressively, by the help of the Holy Spirit, they should become more dedicated to divine purposes as they mature in the Christian life (Phil. 1:6). Of course one cannot talk about this kind of holiness without relating it to Christ.

These holy ones are "in Christ Jesus," joined to Him in living union and communion. The figure of the vine and branches which Christ Himself used in John 15 expresses the relationship clearly. Individual believers as branches draw their life and power to grow and bear fruit from the vine.

Why Paul singles out the "bishops and deacons" in his address can only be guessed. Presumably it is not to strengthen their hand in exercising authority over an unruly and factious congregation. Possibly it is because they took the lead in collecting the gift for Paul. Both of these terms are taken over from a secular context. A bishop (*episkopos*) was a superintendent, an inspector, a magistrate who regulated the sale of provisions and even appears in an inscription as an official in a temple of Apollo (Deissmann, *Bible Studies*, p. 231). So it had a religious significance before its use in the church.

A deacon (*diakonos*) in the secular world was responsible for such welfare duties as dispensing gifts of food and apparently served similarly in the church. Though the term "deacon" is not used in Acts 6, it usually is thought that the office of deacon originated at that time. Bishops are thought commonly to be synonymous with elders but one cannot be dogmatic on this point. Vincent's comment is a judicious one: "The Pauline epistles . . . exhibit church polity in a rudimentary and fluid state in which official designations are not sharply defined, and the offices themselves have not taken permanent and definite shape . . . The terms often overlap or are confused" (*Commentary*, p. 37). In that spirit the Williams translation, "overseers and assistants," might be particularly valid. At any rate, it is clear that both bishops and deacons are in the plural and evidently have risen from the local congregation. There is no hint of a single supervisor having asserted power over them.

The salutation. In verse 2 we have the salutation. "Grace" and "peace" place Greek and Hebrew greetings side by side; the terms occur not only here but also in all the other Pauline epistles. Paul uses common literary forms of the day, but with considerable change. Instead of the usual Greek *chairein*, a purely secular term meaning "greeting," he chooses another word from the same root, *charis,* meaning "grace." The Hebrew *shalom,* "peace," he does not change in form but puts a great deal into it. Grace is the undeserved favor of God toward the sinner which is preeminently expressed in the provision of salvation through the work of Christ. As Titus 2:11 puts it, "For the grace of God has appeared, bringing salvation to all men" (NASB). Though *shalom,* the Hebrew greeting, came first in order of time, the Greek "grace" takes precedence in Christian truth. God must extend His grace before there can be any peace with God, before there can be any reconciliation. And of course the grace of God must be operative in the individual life before the peace of God can flood the individual soul. The ultimate source of these spiritual blessings is "God our Father and the Lord Jesus Christ."

B. THANKSGIVING AND PRAYER FOR ALL (1:3-11)

Thanksgiving and love for the Philippians. In all of Paul's letters, except Galatians (where he deals with a serious defection from the gospel), he begins with thanksgiving and praise to God for his readers. Certainly Paul has much to be thankful for when he writes the Philippians because God had wonderfully established the church there and they have generously supported him. He would have been ungrateful indeed not to have appeared thankful when writing them. But it is a measure of the apostle's greatness and spiritual maturity for him to be so grateful and joyful throughout this letter when his enemies are doing what they can to make life miserable for him (chap. 1), and when he has now been in prison for most of four years. One must not read the comforts of some modern American prisons back into the Roman world.

Verse 3 is rendered properly with the New American Standard Version, "I thank my God in all my remembrance of you." Thus it indicates that whenever Paul thinks of these friends he gives thanks to God. All that he remembers about them is one pleasant memory and it is cause for thanks to God. Such an observation gives rise to a double question. Do we on the one hand live in such a way as to cause others to give thanks for us, or do we on the other hand live such a self-centered life with such a critical spirit that we cannot be thankful for others? The fact that Paul can utter such effusive thanks for the Philippians does not of course mean that there are no problems among them. Something already has been said about disunity in the Philippian church and more will be said later about this and attendant difficulties. Yet the apostle is able to see beyond present imperfections and to view the Philippians as trophies of divine grace, as true converts who have expressed their faith in God in a tangible way with offerings for his support, and as growing Christians on the way to a higher plane of development (1:6).

In verse 4 Paul's thanksgiving naturally moves into petition: "always in every petition of mine making request for you all with joy."* Thanks and petition go together and thanks normally should precede requests. Of course sometimes our hearts are so burdened with our needs or the needs of others that we launch directly into petition. But even in the midst of agonizing request, prayer will not be the effective experience it ought to be if there is no appreciation of the goodness and character of God or of the benefits He so often has bestowed. Paul assures the Philippians that he is continually making (present participle) entreaty or supplication on their behalf. The prayer is comprehensive, for "you all." He declares his concern for all alike — every child and faulty member — and does not recognize divisiveness or factions. And his intercession on their behalf is offered joyfully. His joy is constant, in spite of all his present difficulties, because of what the Philippians mean to him and of course because of his deep-rooted faith in Christ. Joy is after all a fruit of the Spirit (Gal. 5:22).

The New Testament does not give a specific statement about the prayer life of the apostle Paul, but judging from indications here in verses 3 and 4 and in such passages as Romans 1:9; Colossians 1:3 and 1 Thessalonians 1:2, 3, he must have spent much time in prayer on behalf of the fledgling churches making their way in the Roman world. The Book of Acts pictures Paul primarily as a man on the go, but the epistles intimate that he was a man of deep sensitivity, profound intellectual ability, abounding faith, and constant fellowship with God.

"For your fellowship in the gospel" (v. 5) should be connected with the thanksgiving of verse 3 instead of the asking of verse 4. In other words, verse 5 gives the basis or ground of his thanksgiving: their fellowship in the gospel. The New American Standard Bible gives a helpful translation: "I thank my God . . . in view

*Translations in this commentary are those of the writer, unless otherwise designated.

of your participation in the gospel . . ." (vv. 3, 5). The word here translated "fellowship" or "participation" is *koinōnia,* which has become so popular and has been used so loosely in recent years. The basic meaning in Paul's day was "participation in something with someone," but as usual he gives a greater richness to this word than his secular contemporaries. It does not signify merely a friendly atmosphere in a group or even a bond joining Christians together. In Paul's teaching it involves sharing a common possession, a common mutual interest and a common objective, which includes but goes beyond mere subjective experience. So it is not just a spirit of fellowship but also joint participation in labor, sufferings, enjoyment, and material good.

"Your fellowship" is not "my fellowship with you" nor "your fellowship with me" but "your fellowship with each other" in the work of the gospel. *Koinōnia* in this case is not then mutual interaction or enjoyment of the blessings of the gospel but joint association in an objective work: the furtherance of the gospel. Instead of merely sending thanks for a gift of money, the apostle expresses appreciation on a much higher plane and includes all their cooperation effort to spread the good news of salvation. No doubt he means to include their gift to him as part of that expression of their joint efforts. He praises the Philippians because their *koinōnia* had been constant, from the "first day," the day when they received the gospel, until that moment.

And Paul has absolute confidence that the good things God has been doing for the Philippians He will continue to do. Verse 6 applies to all that has gone before. "Being confident" is in the perfect tense, which means that Paul began long ago to have this certainty and it still continues. "This very thing" simply introduces what follows. "He who began" of course refers to God. As Jonah 2:9 says, "Salvation is of the LORD." That means not only the initial step of justification by faith but all of the intermediate steps of watchcare and growth along the way until the believer appears in the presence of God. "A good work" is not merely the fellowship or *koinōnia* of verse 5, but all that God began to do in them. "Will perfect it" expresses confidence in the certainty that God will consummate or carry through what He has begun. In fact, this good work God will perfect until the "day of Jesus Christ" (see also Phil. 1:10; 2:16; 1 Cor. 1:8; 5:5; 2 Cor. 1:14), probably the day when Christ will return for His church (1 Thess. 4:13-18).

In a general way the verse teaches that God will continue His good work in the heart and life of the believer until the redeemed one stands before Christ whether at death or at His coming. But it is especially at His coming (day of Christ) that the good work God is now doing will be completed and will be fully displayed. What gives Paul this confidence that God will finish what He began? The work God already has done gives assurance of greater things to follow. Blessings already received give hope for the future. He cannot believe that the infinite God of perfection will leave a job half done.

Verse 7˙ gives more specific grounds for the confidence he expresses in verse 6. "It is right for me to think this way about you all." Simple justice demands the confidence that God will finish what He has begun in them. This implies a high level of sincerity and dedication on their part (see 2 Thess. 1:3 for a similar expression). The thought is that their ministry is so exemplary it is just or right to expect that God will continue to bless them. But the real ground of the right mentioned here is the fact that they were all "partakers with me of grace," and it has nothing to do with their conduct or dedication. The undeserved favor of God which caused His smile to rest on Paul had been extended to them also and assures their ultimate enjoyment of His presence. In verse 5 the Philippians had been joint-sharers with Paul in the gospel; here they are joint-sharers with him in the grace of God.

The middle part of verse 7 merely prepares the way for the conclusion. Paul's great love for the Philippian believers colors all his thoughts about them; in fact this love makes his present situation more bearable. It buoys him up while in prison and strengthens him in his defense and confirmation of the gospel before the imperial court. All of them then become not only sharers with him of the grace of God but also shares with him in all the experiences of his ministry.

Although Paul had had only a short personal acquaintance with the Philippians, they had worked themselves deeply into his heart. In verse 8 he expresses how tenderly he holds them in his heart. Unable to verbalize his longing for them, he uses the term "God is my witness," which is somewhat equivalent to saying "God knows the depths of my affection." Maintaining the universality so characteristic of this section, Paul yearns for them "all" with the affection of Christ Jesus. "Affection" or "tender mercies" is in-

elegantly rendered "bowels" in the King James Version. In the
original the word is *splagchnos,* the Greek term for the nobler
viscera (heart, lungs, and liver), from which feelings of love and
tenderness were thought to arise. Paul's affection is not merely
natural in origin; he is so filled with the love of Christ that he
sees Christ as loving through him. This verse reflects Galatians
2:20, "Christ lives in me." Says Lightfoot, ". . . his pulse beats
with the pulse of Christ; his heart throbs with the heart of Christ"
(p. 85).

Prayer for continuing growth. In verses 3-8 Paul has been
pouring out his heart in thanksgiving and love for the Philippians;
now in 9-11 he turns to prayer for their continuing spiritual
growth. "And this I keep on praying: that your love may abound
still more and more." He does not mean to disparage the degree
of love already evident among them but seeks greater depth and
new dimensions of development. "Your love" is their mutual
love for each other, their regard for their fellow man, not specifically their love for Paul.

Love may abound; it may be eager, enthusiastic, and exuberant,
and yet be lacking in knowledge and discernment. Thus misunder-
standings and other difficulties sometimes arise among believers.
Love must be accompanied by "knowledge and perception as its
attendants and aids" (Moule, p. 43). Knowledge here is advanced
knowledge, developed knowledge of the truth, orderly comprehensive acquaintance with something. It is "practical knowledge
which informs Christian love as to right circumstances, aims, ways
and means" (Vincent, *Commentary,* p. 12). "Judgment" (KJV)
is better translated "discernment" or "discrimination," and is
sensitive moral perception or tact. Love regulated by a more
advanced knowledge of God and His ways and by Christian tact
would be an effective antidote to the faultfinding or factionalism
that contributed to disunity in the Philippian church — and for
that matter in any other church. Note that Paul prayed for this
kind of regulated love to develop among Philippian believers
before seeking to administer correction (e.g., 4:2, 3). This lesson
should not be lost on modern churches and pastors.

The knowledge and discernment that comes to the Philippians
in answer to Paul's prayer will enable them to "approve things
that are excellent" (KJV, v. 10). "Approve" may better be translated "test" or "put to the test." The Greek word for "test" is used
of testing money to prove its genuineness. "Things that are ex-

cellent" (KJV) may also be translated "things that differ." The idea is that one will be able to apply tests to differences of view and to make spiritual decisions that the immature believer cannot make. This ability to apply spiritual discrimination comes in large measure from the renewing of the mind (Rom. 12:2) which enables one to prove (*dokimazein* — same word as for "approve" in Phil. 1:10) or put to the test for the purpose of proving the correctness of God's good and acceptable and perfect will. Vincent beautifully captures the whole thought: "May your love increase and abound in ripe knowledge and perceptive power, that you may apply the right tests and reach the right decisions in things which present moral differences" (Vincent, *Commentary,* p. 13).

The purpose or goal of this deeper knowledge and discernment is that believers will "be sincere and blameless until the day of Christ" (NASB). "Sincere" is not an adequate translation because one may go at testing sincerely enough and be sincerely wrong in his beliefs, and because the word no longer has the same significance it once did. Sincere meant "without wax" and designated porcelain that was perfect. Cracked porcelain frequently was patched with wax, and honest merchants who wished to advertise their integrity labeled their wares *sine cera.* The archaic meaning of the word then was pure or unmixed. Reference here is to one who is inwardly pure or unpolluted or genuine through and through. The Williams translation renders it "transparent character." "Blameless" may be translated in an active sense, "without being a cause of stumbling," or passive, "not stumbling," i.e., undamaged or uninjured. Qualified Greek students argue in both directions. In any case one who is inwardly pure should have a blameless outward conduct of life. The concern that one shall live in this exemplary way until the day of Christ underscores the fact that at Christ's coming believers' works will be judged (2 Cor. 5:10) and that the coming of Christ serves as an incentive to right living so one may stand before Him unashamed (1 John 3:2, 3).

A pure and blameless life is more fully defined as "Being filled with the fruits of righteousness" (v. 11). "Fruit of righteousness" comes from the Old Testament (see Prov. 11:30; Amos 6:12; compare James 3:18). Fruit is in the singular in the best manuscripts (as in Phil. 1:22; Gal. 5:22; Eph. 5:9) and is the total product of a holy life or the result of righteousness. Righteousness here is not justification but right conduct. Williams in his translation renders it "right-doing." Of course it is impossible to divorce a display of ethical conduct from right relation to God. Standardly in Scripture good works pleasing to God can be performed only after the believer's commitment to God. Ability to perform good works or bear fruit is possible only for the branch that is in the vine and drawing upon the life of the vine (John 15:4). Put another way, these acts of right-doing are not a product of the individual believer in his own energy but are fruit of the Spirit (Gal. 5:22, 23). And of course it is made clear in this verse that right conduct comes "through Jesus Christ." Moreover, any success we may have in living an exemplary life and doing good works is not to our own glory but "to the glory and praise of God" (see Eph. 1:6, 12, 14). Mounce aptly observes, "The goal of all Christian activity is to bring recognition and homage to the divine perfections of a redeeming God" (p. 1322).

FOR FURTHER STUDY

1. If you regarded yourself as merely a steward of Jesus Christ, how would that change your view of the Christian life?

2. What hints do you discover concerning the prayer life of Paul in Acts 9-28?

3. On the basis of what is said about *koinōnia* in the discussion of verses 5 and 6, what do you think the Koinōnia group in your church should be like?

4. What tests would you apply to determine a right decision concerning things which present moral differences (v. 10)?

5. Compare the prayer of Paul for the Philippians with his prayers for the Colossians and Ephesians, written from prison about the same time. Note the leading requests in each and compare them.

CHAPTER 4

Paul's Imprisonment as Related to the Question of Unity

(Phil. 1:12-30)

To calm the fears and concerns of the Philippians over his present situation, Paul now turns to a discussion of his affairs. It is no sob story. Nor does he dwell on details of life in prison. Rather he leaves us with many questions about how things really were. His uppermost concern is with the gospel and its advance. In spite of the fact that he is imprisoned and not free to preach, in spite of the fact that enemies in the local church where he is (presumably Rome) are trying to make life miserable for him, he rejoices that the gospel is being preached. Perhaps his spirit of optimism is due in part also to a belief that his imprisonment is near an end. Presumably his case has had a preliminary hearing and he has learned that acquittal will come soon. One may infer this from 1:25, 26 where he expresses an absolute certainty that his life will be spared and that he will see them again.

Something should be said here about the theme of unity as developed in chapter 1. Evidently there is disunity in the church at Rome. This may be inferred from some of the motivation that spurs them on to preaching the gospel. He tolerates this factionalism because in spite of it the work of the gospel is advanced (vv. 12-18). In verses 19-26 he discusses the possibility that he may be removed from earthly ministry but finally concludes that he will be preserved to help insure the Philippians' growth in grace. Of course that growth would retard or destroy disunity among them. Then in the closing verses of the chapter he issues an exhortation to unity among them while he remains in prison for a while.

A. TOLERATION OF DISUNITY IN MOTIVES FOR EVANGELISTIC WORK (1:12-18).

With Paul in prison it would seem that the gospel ministry might be greatly hindered. But the apostle reports this is not the case. Actually the ministry is progressing at a considerable rate.

Although some factious individuals preach with inferior or impure motives, he does not attack them but rejoices instead because the cause of Christ is going forward.

Perhaps the Philippians had sent either a written or oral message by Epaphroditus (2:25) inquiring about Paul's prison experience. In reply he says, "I wish you to know [come to know, learn, or understand] brothers [fellow believers who are members of the same spiritual family by faith in Christ] that my circumstances [that is, recent developments in his case] have turned out rather [in contrast to what might be expected] unto the advancement of the gospel." "Advancement" means literally to "cut before" and introduces the idea of pioneers cutting a path before an army to facilitate its march. This figure of speech, like so many others in the book, would appeal to the Roman veterans at Philippi. The gospel is on the march in hearts and hands and on the lips of believers, and the gates of hell shall not be able to stand against it (Matt. 16:18).

Paul doesn't even hint at the hardships amidst his circumstances but simply rejoices over the spread of the good news about what Jesus Christ has done for man. Paul had learned to rejoice in Christ in the midst of adversity (2 Cor. 12:10) and to be content with his lot in life (Phil. 4:11). It is entirely possible, as Kennedy suggests, that a major change had occurred recently in Paul's circumstances: a transfer from minimum security conditions (Acts 28:30) to a maximum security prison for individuals actually on trial. Now he would not have the freedom to preach and the work of the gospel would be curtailed. Just the opposite had happened (p. 423).

His imprisonment had become known not as a matter of notoriety but as connected with Christ's cause and endured for Christ's sake (v. 13). It was not a result of any breach of law. As Paul was able constantly to hammer home this truth to his guards, the gospel gradually permeated the entire Praetorium (KJV, "palace"). What the Praetorium is here has caused considerable debate. Elsewhere in Scripture it may refer to the residence of a provincial governor or client king (Matt. 27:27; Mark 15:16; John 18:28, 33; 19:9; Acts 23:35) and may be synonymous with government house. Apparently there is no sufficient authority for applying it here to the emperor's palace, the barracks near the palace, or the camp of the Praetorian Guard, but refers instead to the guard itself (Lightfoot, pp. 99-104). The

New American Standard Bible translation, "throughout the whole praetorian guard," is satisfactory.

The situation is this. Upon arrival in Rome Paul was turned over to the Praetorian Prefect, the commander of the imperial guards, and apparently remained under his supervision until his release. Henceforth he was handcuffed to a member of the guard. The Greek of Ephesians 6:20 and Acts 28:20 mentions these coupling-chains. Incarceration was not in a dungeon maintained by the state but in quarters that Paul paid for himself (Acts 28:30). Naturally, as Paul's guards rotated over a two-year period he had a chance to witness to a number of them. And of course many heard him discuss the Christian faith with his visitors. Some guards no doubt made profession of faith and discussed Paul's message with other members of the Praetorian Guard. Even those who did not become Christians could not have failed to be impressed by this unusual prisoner. Thus the gospel had permeated the elite guard of the Empire (some 9,000 strong). This fact certainly would have impressed and rejoiced the old army men in the church at Philippi.

"In all other places" (KJV) is properly translated "to all the rest" and cannot be applied too specifically. It simply refers to a wide circle in Rome beyond the guard itself. No doubt it included members of the Emperor's palace staff (Phil. 4:22). Support for Paul's contention that knowledge of Christianity was becoming widespread in Rome is found in the Roman historian Tacitus who said that by the time Nero began to persecute Christians (A.D. 64, less than five years after Paul wrote Philippians) there was a "vast multitude" of them in Rome (Ellicott, p. 216).

Not only had Paul's imprisonment resulted in a witness for Christ in governmental circles in Rome, but it also had stimulated believers there to greater evangelistic activity. "Most [not 'many' as in the KJV] of the brethren growing confident in the Lord because of my imprisonment are more abundantly bold to speak the word of God without fear" (v. 14). The few who were not inspired by Paul's imprisonment were either his opponents mentioned in verse 15 or individuals who were frightened by the possible consequences of witness. The "growing confidence in the Lord" was encouraged as they saw in Paul the power and sufficient grace of Christ. In this way Christ was magnified in Paul's body (v. 20).

Variety of motives for preaching. Now Paul seems to divide the preaching brethren of verse 14 into two groups: those who preach from worthy motives and from unworthy motives. Clearly all are believers. He is not trying to distinguish between believers and heretics, or even between those who are doctrinally correct and those who are guilty of slight errors in doctrine. The dividing issue is correctness of motive.

Some preached because of envy and strife. They were envious of Paul because God had given him greater gifts and because he had been so successful in his ministry in the capital. He was the topic of conversation throughout the Praetorian Guard and in the streets of the city, and even among some of the Emperor's palace. They would show him a thing or two. They would preach with such vigor as to draw attention away from him and gain proper recognition for themselves.

"Strife" is factious rivalry. Some proclaimed Christ with "selfishness" (KJV, "contention"; NASB, "selfish ambition," v. 16), with the self-seeking of a hired worker laboring only for his own interests, "not purely" (KJV, "sincerely"). Their motivation was impure; the allusion in the Greek text is to precious metal mixed with a base alloy. They thought that by winning converts and gaining influence in the church they would annoy Paul; he would feel even more the limitations of his imprisonment when he was unable to move around and deal with this opposition to him. "To add affliction to my bonds," in the Greek, is an action of painful rubbing of iron chains on a prisoner's arms and legs. The successful preaching of the preachers would supposedly irritate him as he lay helpless in prison, but it was hollow pretense (v. 18), devoid of reality, and he treated it as such.

Others preached Christ out of the motivation of "good will" (v. 15), a desire for the good of others, in this case, Paul. Love is the source of their action (v. 17). This love is regulated by true knowledge and spiritual perception (v. 9). These brethren "have come to know that I am set for the defense of the gospel" (v. 17). They understand that God has put Paul in his present position in the church and that his imprisonment is a result of his faithful service to Christ, not of self-seeking ambition or a run-in with civil law. "I am set" or "appointed" or "positioned" (*keimai*) is a military term. As a good soldier of Jesus Christ he was set for the defense of the gospel. "Defense" is a legal term and perhaps here is a reference to his legal trial. These Christians do not proclaim Christ with unworthy ulterior motives but in sincerity and truth (v. 18) — their actions truly reflect their inner attitudes.

Paul's reaction to inferior motives for preaching. As Paul looks at the factional development in the Roman community, he says in effect, "So what? What is my reaction to all this?" ("What then?"). His answer is, "only that ['notwithstanding,' KJV] in every way [from whatever motives] whether in pretense [with a counterfeited zeal or with a mask covering real motives] or in truth [with pure motives], Christ is preached." In this fact the apostle rejoices and will continue to rejoice. Instead of making life miserable for Paul, his enemies have made him glad.

It is clear here that the factious preachers are not proclaiming a false gospel for that would bring no joy to Paul. There is nothing wrong with the substance of their message but rather with the motivation that leads them to preach it. It is important to underscore this point. Paul is absolutely intolerant of heresy which becomes crystal clear from his denunciation of anyone who preaches "another [false] gospel." (See for instance, Gal. 1:9: "let him be accursed.") But he is reasonably tolerant of one who in a condition of spiritual immaturity or even through base motivation carries on the work of Christ. What matters most is that the work of Christ goes on, not that Paul is running the show or even that he is physically comfortable.

B. PAUL'S PRESERVATION TO PROMOTE A CONTINUATION OF THEIR GROWTH IN GRACE (1:19-26).

Apparently verses 19-26 reflect Paul's thinking as he faces his trial in Rome. He is concerned especially that whether the outcome is life or death for him Christ will be honored. And he recognizes that the decision in the case will affect not only himself but the Philippians as well. Seemingly a preliminary hearing gives him the absolute confidence that he will be released. Therefore he will be able to minister to the Philippians in person again. Such ministry will contribute to their growth in spiritual maturity and hence will lead to greater unity among believers there.

Paul's concern over his testimony. "For I know that this shall eventuate in my salvation" (v. 19) is a passage with major problems of interpretation. "Know" *(oida)* is intuitive or absolute knowledge, knowledge of settled conviction. But what "this" and "salvation" refer to is quite another matter. Some think "this" refers to the fact that Christ is being preached, but it is not clear how such activity might eventuate or end in Paul's salvation, particularly if one properly understands what the salvation is. It seems better to refer "this" to his present situation in its entirety or the present state of things. "Salvation" here can hardly refer to salvation from eternal damnation nor the whole saving and sanctifying work of Christ in the believer (which is already assured for Paul), nor even Paul's release from prison, because the result will be the same whether he lives or dies (v. 20). It seems rather to refer to the vindication of his stand for Christ and his being saved from disgracing the gospel as he moves through the stages of his trial. Several commentators note the fact that Paul's wording for "this shall end in my salvation" is identical to the Septuagint (Greek) translation of Job 13:16. Job sought the same kind of vindication of his integrity (see Job 13:18) that Paul sought in Rome.

Paul already had stated in Philippians 1:7 that the Philippians were partakers with him in the defense and confirmation of the gospel (legal terms in the Greek). Now he says that this salvation or vindication will come about through the prayers of the Philippians and the supply of the Spirit of Jesus Christ. One article links these two sources of deliverance in the Greek. Paul rests heavily on the effectual prayers of the church, joining them with the work of the Holy Spirit. What he expects the Holy Spirit to supply in answer to prayer is intimated in such passages as Matthew 10:19, 20 and Mark 13:10: He will put the right answer into the mouth of the believer as he stands before earthly judges. Of course the idea is not that in answer to prayer Paul would have more of the Holy Spirit, for the Spirit comes to indwell believers at the moment of salvation (Rom. 8:9-16). Henceforth believers are called upon to permit the Spirit to assume full control (filling of the Spirit) of their lives (Eph. 5:18), not to pray for more of the Spirit. In other words, as we grow more spiritual, we do not get more of the Spirit but He gets more of us.

As something of a confirmation of the interpretation of "salvation" adopted above, in verse 20 Paul expresses the concern that in nothing he shall be "ashamed" or better, "put to shame." It is his "earnest expectation and hope" that this will be the case. "Earnest expectation" is a magnificent word in the Greek. Actually it is a compound of three words which pictures an individual watching with head outstretched and attention focused in a state of maximum alert. "Nothing" refers to no point or respect. Moving now from a negative to a more positive approach ("but"), Paul expresses the confidence that with all "boldness" or unreserved speech, with a courage in his whole being that Christ shall now, "as always" (a modest reference to his flawless testimony in the past) be magnified or exalted in his body. The idea is not that Paul himself will magnify Christ but that his body will be the locality in which Christ will be magnified. This exaltation can come as in the midst of suffering and weakness a divine peace and joy floods his whole personality. It can come either in facing the continuing vicissitudes of life or in a courageous facing of death.

Verse 21 enlarges on the last words of verse 20. Christ could be magnified or exalted by Paul's life or his death because "to me to live is Christ, and to die is gain." Christ is all to him, he lives only to serve Christ, he has no conception of life apart from Christ, he is almost literally one with Christ. Christ's goals, Christ's orientation to life and society and mission, are his. Christ lives out His life through him. Death could not break that union either. In fact it would be gain because it would mean being with Christ (v. 23), receiving a crown of righteousness (2 Tim. 4:8), a fuller development of the life of Christ in him as the old nature was removed (see Rom. 7:15-25), and an end to his physical sufferings (2 Cor. 11:23-28). This is a tremendous verse, not to be taken lightly on the lips or quoted glibly by some carnal or immature Christian who wants to have something impressive to say in a testimony meeting.

Paul's struggle over remaining or departing. Verse 22 connects with "to live" in verse 21. The Greek is difficult and reflects the conflict going on in Paul's mind between the desire to serve Christ on earth and the longing to be united with Christ in heaven. Though it requires addition of a couple of words for smoothness of diction, the rendering of the first part of the verse probably should be, "If I am to go on living in the flesh." The next construction is translated literally, "this to me fruit of work," and probably implies that if he goes on living, he will keep on working for God; this continued work will bear good fruit. In such an event he says, "What I shall choose I do not say." Standardly in the New Testament the Greek word here rendered "know" ("wot") means "to declare" or "make known." Vincent well expresses the meaning of the verse, "If I am assured that my continuing to live is most fruitful for the Church, then I say nothing as to my personal preference. I do not declare my choice. It is not for me to express a choice" (*Word Studies,* p. 424).

Paul's struggle elaborated. Paul's struggle is elaborated on in verses 23 and 24. "I am held fast from the two [sides]." He is hemmed in as it were, pressed from both sides. On the one hand he has a strong desire or impulse to depart because death provides entrance into the immediate presence of Christ. The apostle clearly teaches that the state following death is not an unconscious experience or purgatorial discipline but immediate enjoyment of the presence of Christ. Paul's emphasis is not on rest from labors or escape from the hardships of life (as is the case with many) but on being with Christ. To describe that experience he heaps up words which mean literally, "much more better," but are properly translated "far better" or "much better."

The word translated "depart" is a beautiful expression for death. It is a military term referring to breaking camp or a nautical expression for releasing a ship from its moorings. It may be rendered literally "loosing away upward," and in contemporary experience could refer to a great balloon or dirigible ready for launching and straining at its cables, waiting to be loosed from its moorings so it could fly away. This same word appears in Paul's "valedictory" in 2 Timothy 4:6, where some years later he said, "My loosing away upward is at hand."

While Paul may be straining to get away to heaven, there is a heavy weight holding him down: the needs of believers. To return to the figure introduced at the beginning of verse 23, while he may be pressed on the one hand by the desire to go to be with Christ, he is pressed on the other hand by the realization of the needs of fledgling believers for help and encouragement to meet the tests of life. As a good shepherd of his many flocks, Paul carried on his shoulders daily the heavy weight of the care of the churches (2 Cor. 11:28).

Certainty of continued stay on earth. As we move into verse 25 the tone seems to change. Instead of a conflict over whether to leave or stay, instead of uncertainty about the future, Paul expresses a new confidence and certainty. "Being confident of this" presumably refers to his realization that it is more important at the moment for him to remain on earth. How Paul knew what his immediate future would be is not clear. Perhaps he had had a preliminary legal hearing and was now sure of acquittal. Possibly God clearly revealed it to him or maybe it was a settled intuitive conviction. At any rate, he is sure that he will remain on earth and that he will enjoy prolonged association with "all" the Christians at Philippi — another reference to the unity and corporate nature of the body of believers there. This continued association with them was not for their mutual social enjoyment but for their "furtherance and joy of faith." This may be interpreted variously as progress in the Christian life based on a deepening of joy and an enlargement of faith, or progress in the Christian life and joy which accompanies growth or, perhaps better, for promoting their faith and joy in believing.

Paul's remaining on earth and continued association with the Philippians is to the end that their "exultation may abound in Christ Jesus" (v. 26). While the ground of the exultation is Christ, the occasion would be "in me, through my presence with you again." That is to say, Paul's release from prison would be an occasion of great joy as he had a chance to rehearse before them God's gacious dealings with him during imprisonment. In a real sense "Christ will be magnified in my body" (v. 20). Beet aptly observes, "Paul's presence once more at Philippi after his imprisonment will give to the Christians there in his person an increased confidence and exultation in Christ. Thus will his continued life increase his readers' faith in God, and consequently their joy and their spiritual growth" (p. 53).

C. EXHORTATION TO UNITY WHILE PAUL REMAINS IN PRISON FOR A TIME (1:27-30).

Although Paul fully expects to see the Philippians again and to minister to them in person, that ministry will have to be deferred temporarily. Meanwhile an exhortation to Christian maturity and steadfastness is in order. Literally translated, the first part of verse 27 would read, "Only be citizens [or exercise your citizenship] worthy of the Gospel of Christ." "Only" — this one thing he urges upon them especially. A reference to citizenship would appeal to Romans in the colony of Philippi because they were proud of this privileged status and prized the rights and benefits that went with it. This reference would appeal especially to them on this occasion because another Roman citizen is writing them from the capital of the Empire and sends greetings from the household of Caesar. Of course he is applying the term to a Christian commonwealth rather than a secular, political commonwealth.

To act their part as citizens or to exercise their citizenship would involve shouldering their duties or responsibilities as well as enjoying their rights. The New American Standard Version expresses the thought accurately: "Only conduct yourselves in a manner worthy of the gospel of Christ." It is interesting to note that in Paul's only other use of this verb (Acts 23:1)* he claims to have lived worthily as a good citizen of this heavenly commonwealth. Paul does not at this juncture spell out what conducting one's self in a manner worthy of the gospel of Christ might involve. No doubt it would include all the kinds of things he urges upon the Romans, Corinthians, Thessalonians, Colossians, Ephesians, Galatians, and the Philippians later in this letter, as part of Christian maturity. Of course it would be impossible for him to go into that kind of detail here.

But some aspects of this worthy conduct are highlighted in the remaining verses of chapter 1. Initially he encourages their exemplary conduct so he may have the joy or encouragement of hearing about their Christian progress. The result would be the same whether he comes to visit them or hears by way of a report of others. This injection of uncertainty about visiting them does not contradict his certainty in verse 25 that he will continue to live on earth for a while, because if his life were not spared he could neither visit nor hear about them.

What did Paul want to hear about them? What would constitute worthy conduct? That they "stand fast" in an unyielding maintenance of their testimony "in one spirit, with one mind." Here is a direct appeal to Christian unity. The "one spirit" is not the Holy Spirit but a disposition or attitude that is the fruit of the ministry of the Holy Spirit in their lives. The "mind" or "soul" is the seat of the sensations or desires or affections; and the "one mind" would involve a united front, not weakened by internal rivalries. "Striving together for the faith" is not striving along with Paul but in teamwork with each other. The Beck translation properly puts it: "fighting side by side like one man." The imagery is that of an athletic or gladiatorial contest in which a team is grappling with its opponents in a herculean struggle. The object of the struggle is to maintain the faith of the gospel: in this case the body of truth committed to the church. As is clear from the following verse, this faith is to be maintained against adversaries who deny the faith.

*The word is buried in the clause "I have lived in all good conscience."

As they close ranks and fight together in a show of united effort, the Philippians are not to be frightened (as a terrified horse is startled and stampedes, is the picture in the Greek text) out of a compact and effective battle array. "Adversaries" who might strike fear into them were in Philippi almost certainly Gentiles because Jews were so few in number there. Presumably they were stirring up the same kind of mob violence that had landed Paul and Silas in the Philippian jail at the time the church was founded (Acts 16). At least that is the intimation of verse 30 where Paul refers to the conflict he faced among them while in Philippi. The antecedent of "which" is their fearlessness. This courageous stance will be an "evidence" or "proof" to their persecutors of their destruction or loss of eternal life. It will show that they cannot destroy God's work and that fighting against it can only bring about their destruction.

And, of course, the ability to stand in the face of persecution is not a product of human determination but is a result of the working of the Holy Spirit in lives of believers (see Mark 13:11). Such divine enablement should provide evidence for the Philippians, and all other Christians, that they are true believers — that they possess eternal salvation. To what "and that from God" refers is difficult to say with certainty. Probably it refers to the "evidence" of salvation or "courage" as coming from God, but in the light of verse 29 it also may indicate that the persecution came in the sovereign purpose of God.

The reason why the Philippians (and others) should not be thrown into utter confusion and dismay by persecution appears in verse 29: "For to you it has been granted [freely bestowed as a gracious gift] on behalf of Christ." Suffering for Christ's sake is to be viewed as a privilege. As God has bestowed the gift of salvation so he also has bestowed the gift of suffering. If faith brings oneness with Christ, then the believer must expect to share not only the glory of Christ's relationship with the Father, but also the fierceness of His opposition among men. Jesus Himself said, "If the world hate you, ye know that it hated me before it hated you" (John 15:18). It should be clear from this verse that much suffering Christians endure is not because of their sin or even their foolishness, but because of allegiance to Christ. It is an accompaniment of the Christian faith and even may be viewed as a sign of God's favor and an evidence of His salvation.

Just as the Philippians had been partakers with Paul in grace

(1:7), so now they are partakers with him in suffering (v. 30). They were experiencing the same conflict or same sort of conflict or suffering they saw him face in Philippi and now learned he was facing in Rome. The word for "conflict" (agōn) generally applied to athletic contests or struggles in the arena. Why should Paul bother to observe that the Philippians and he were facing the same sort of opposition — were in the same boat together, so to speak?

In the first place, he already has observed that suffering for Christ is a concomitant of the Christian faith and is an evidence of one's salvation. He had had his share of persecution as a proof of his salvation and they can likewise expect their share. Second, as they saw him face persecution in Philippi, they saw him undaunted by it. Likewise they had now in the epistle he was writing and from the mouth of Epaphroditus word that he was not buckling under the pressure of opposition in Rome either. This should be a special encouragement to them to "stand fast" (v. 27). Such steadfastness would be an evidence of their salvation and would be an important part of acting like citizens of the Christian commonwealth (v. 27).

FOR FURTHER STUDY

1. Draw up lists of worthy and unworthy motives for preaching the gospel or serving Christ (for they are synonymous). Which of these have spurred you on?

2. Paul rejoiced because though some of his opponents had meant to do him ill, the cause of the gospel was advanced. How tolerant should we be of what we consider to be wrong ways of doing the work of Christ, or of evil if good comes of it?

3. If you were to say, "To me to live is Christ," what would that statement mean to you?

4. What does Paul have to say in Ephesians about living in a manner worthy of the gospel of Christ? Note the exhortations to "walk" in a certain manner.

5. What would "striving together for the faith" require of a group of modern American believers?

CHAPTER 5

The Mind of Christ:
The Source of All Unity

(Phil. 2:1-30)

A magnificent demonstration of the fact that the mind of Christ is the source of all unity is the theme of this chapter. Following an exhortation to harmony comes one of the most significant doctrinal passages in all of Scripture, one which shows the essential nature of the mind of Christ. Next appears the product of the mind of Christ in the church and then a statement about examples of those who possess the mind of Christ: Paul, Timothy, and Epaphroditus.

A. NATURE: HUMILITY OF SPIRIT (2:1-11)

1. *Exhortation to Unity Based on the Mind of Christ* (2:1-4).

Paul's appeal at the beginning of this chapter is clearly an expansion on the exhortation to unity begun in 1:27. The "exercise of citizenship" in a way becoming the gospel involves not only standing for the faith in a spirit of unity against external adversaries but also maintenance of inner harmony in the fellowship of believers to enhance the witness and effectiveness of the group. The fourfold basis of appeal in verse 1 is expressed in "if" clauses in English (conditional clauses which assume the fact to be true). Actually there is no doubt in the apostle's mind, and "since" may be substituted properly at the beginning of each clause. "Consolation" is better rendered "exhortation" and probably Vincent has captured the significance in his expanded translation: "If the fact of your being in Christ has any power to exhort you to brotherly concord" (*Commentary*, p. 53). "Comfort of love" (KJV) may be translated better as "persuasion" or "persuasive power of love." What love is in view cannot be determined for certain. It could be Paul's love for them, their love for each other, their love for Paul, or Christ's love for the church.

"Fellowship of the Spirit" could be fellowship wrought by the Spirit or fellowship with or participation in the Spirit. In either

case, the fact of the Holy Spirit's ministry to believers ought to
deal the death blow to factiousness. He baptizes believers into one
body when they put their faith in Christ (1 Cor. 12:3). He in-
dwells believers and works in their hearts and lives to bring them
into greater conformity to Christ and thus to greater unity of the
fellowship. And of course the fruit of the Spirit (Gal. 5:22, 23)
will promote unity of the brethren.

"Bowels and mercies" (KJV) is better rendered "tenderhearted-
ness and sympathy" as in the Williams translation. Bowels were
looked on as the seat of the emotions and in this case would
refer to an inner state. Sympathy would indicate an outward expression of feeling. Whether God's tender compassion for the
church in its need, or the apostle's pastoral concern, or the tender
concern one Christian ought to have for another is in view, need
not be decided. All of them would be important for restoring unity.
Though Paul's message here is a powerful basis for solving the
problems facing the Philippian church, it rings through the corri-
dors of time to deal with party strife everywhere.

Paul's joy would be complete if his readers would yield to his
plea for unity (v. 2). And he heaps up phrases to underscore the
intensity of his request. "Likeminded" is to think the same thing,
to be compelled by the same aims and objectives. "Same love"
refers to a mutual love, the one love of God in all. "Of one
accord" is "with united souls" and involves a harmony of feeling
and affections. "Of one mind" repeats what already has been said
but is a slightly stronger expression than "likeminded."

In verse 3 "nothing" stands alone in the Greek without a verb.
While most translators supply "doing," it would be just as appropriate to supply "thinking," connecting with the previous verse
which puts emphasis on motivation behind action. "Through
strife" (KJV) is literally "according to faction" or "by way of
faction" and focuses on faction or contention as a regulative
principle according to which something is done. "Vainglory" or
vanity or seeking after vain glory involves any vain or erroneous
thinking about one's self, and is the opposite of giving proper
glory to God.

In contrast to factiousness and seeking after vain glory, Paul
urges a true humility before God which recognizes the dependence of the creature on the Creator and the placement of all men
on the same level before God. Moreover, one is encouraged to
recognize some of the strong points of his neighbor that might

excel some of his own capabilities. Passages of this sort frequently are misunderstood. Some erroneously put on a false humility and engage in a destructive self-effacement. This is not biblical. We have every right and responsibility to discover and cultivate our God-given gifts (1 Tim. 4:14; 2 Tim. 1:6). But at the same time, for our own proper humility, for the encouragement of others and the most effective operation of the body of Christ, we need to recognize that others can do many things better than we can and we must give them the proper honor and encouragement in the performance of their gifts.

Verse 4 completes the thought of the latter part of verse 3. One is not to esteem or fix his attention ("look") only on his own things or concerns or even development of his own spiritual gifts, but is also to focus attention on or recognize the good qualities of fellow Christians.

2. *The Mind of Christ in Action: Obedient Even Unto Death* (2:5-8).

Having delivered another eloquent appeal for unity in the first four verses of the chapter, Paul now introduces Christ as the ultimate example of true humility, as one who had the sort of mind set that would bring about a blessed unity in the body of believers. Although this is an intensely practical passage, it is one of the most important doctrinal statements in all of Scripture. The presence of such elevated truths here helps to demonstrate the fact that practice must be founded on doctrine and is constantly related to it. Those who say they are not interested in theology but stick to the simple truths of Christian living taught in Scripture over-look the fact that the Bible itself makes doctrine foundational to all Christian action. And, of course, a proper formulation of theology is simply an organization of the truths of Scripture in a more formal way. If our theology is merely human jargon that does not give proper recognition to Scripture, it does not deserve to be honored as theology.

"Let this mind be in you" (v. 5, KJV) involves an exhortation to have the same mind set or attitude as Christ had when He left heaven's glory to assume human form and all the humiliation connected with his earthly life and death. Actually, the preferred reading of the first part of the verse would be "keep on having this mind in you," which may imply the necessity of vigilance in maintaining an orientation to life that could be eroded easily.

"In you" does not indicate that the mind of Christ would come to dwell in them to impart some special virtue, but rather his attitude of self-abnegation would so permeate the body of believers individually and collectively that strife would cease. Beck translates the verse crisply and effectively: "Think just as Christ Jesus thought."

How did Christ think? Verses 6-8 give the answer. Christ "being" or "existing" or "subsisting" is a translation from a word that indicates prior existence, what He was before He took on human flesh. At that time He was in the "form" (*morphē*) of God. To an English reader "form" has something to do with shape or outward appearance. And outward appearance often may be quite different from the real nature of something. But the Greek word used here implies identification of form with essence or nature, answering to it in every particular. The last half of verse 6 is difficult but the Williams translation gives a good approximation: "He did not think His being on an equality with God a thing to be selfishly grasped." Similarly, Walvoord interprets, "He did not hold the outer manifestation of His deity as a treasure that had to be grasped and retained" (p. 53).

Having a mind set like that, Christ in humility "made himself of no reputation," literally "emptied Himself; taking the form of a bondservant" (NASB). It is important to recognize that Christ freely of His own volition performed this condescending act and became man. There has been endless theological speculation over the significance of emptying (*ekenōsen*). Many have taught that He actually laid aside one or more qualities of deity. But if Christ gave up even one of His divine attributes, He would be no longer God. There is no hint in this passage or anywhere else in Scripture that Christ gave up any aspects of His deity, but in becoming man He did limit the exercise or manifestation of His deity. Lightfoot described Christ's action in *ekenōsen* as " 'emptied, stripped *Himself*' of the insignia of majesty" (p. 112), and that must be an approximation of what is intended here.

Christ's emptying is defined or amplified in the rest of verse 7 and verse 8. He took the form of a bondservant. The word for "form" is the same as in verse 6. "He became *really* and *essentially* the servant of men" (Luke 22:27) (Vincent, *Word Studies*, p. 433). "Being made [literally 'becoming'] in the likeness of men," He *became* something He was not. He took on the *likeness* of men. He was like man in that He had a body that looked like man and acted like man and really was man.

Yet He was different; it is not said here that He took the *morphē* of man. In His likeness He was not identical with man. In the words of Hebrews 4:15, as a man He could be "touched with the feeling of our infirmities" but He was "without sin." As a person not plagued by the sin nature, He did not think or act quite like other human beings. In spite of the distinction, it could be said He was truly God and truly man. As Walvoord observes, "the form of a servant was superimposed upon His deity without taking away His divine attributes. He was like a king who temporarily puts on the garments of a peasant while at the same time remaining king . . . " (p. 54).

"Being found in appearance as a man," having the characteristics of a man or recognized by man's senses as being really a man, He suffered further and complete humiliation by subjecting Himself to death, "even the death of the cross." This form of death was the climax of humiliation, reserved by the Romans for common criminals and slaves. The cross was a stumbling block to the Jews because of the curse levied against it (Gal. 3:13; Deut. 21:23) and foolishness to the Greeks (1 Cor. 1:23) who associated all forms of grace and beauty with their deities — certainly not gory death as a criminal. For a greater appreciation of the true humiliation of Christ in His sufferings and death, one should read the passion accounts in each of the four gospels, Psalm 22, and Isaiah 53.

Of special significance to Paul's argument in Philippians 2 is the fact that Christ *voluntarily* emptied Himself, took the form of a bondservant, and humbled Himself to the death of the cross. As He Himself said, "I lay down my life, that I might take it again. No man taketh it from me, but I lay it down of myself. I have power to lay it down, and I have power to take it again" (John 10:17, 18). He never lost His full deity, but "He did not think His being on an equality with God a thing to be selfishly grasped." He did not merely look out for His own personal interests, but also for the interests of others (Phil. 2:4). Christ's attitude of complete self-abnegation was the special truth Paul had in mind when he encouraged the Philippians to think as Christ thought (v. 5). If they did, all petty squabbles and factionalism in their midst would cease. And in line with the observation made earlier about the connection of doctrine and practical Christianity,

the impact of His self-abnegation for the good of others is lost if
He was not preexistent and divine and if He did not become truly
human.

3. *Exaltation by the Father* (2:9-11).

"Wherefore" or "therefore" (v. 9), in consequence of Christ's
voluntary humiliation, God highly exalted Him. What is involved
in highly exalted (lit., "exalted-beyond," one of the compounds
Paul is so fond of piling up) is debated. Some refer it to the
resurrection, others to the ascension. There seems to be no special
reason why both could not be possible. But of course full exaltation could not be revealed until Christ returned to heaven to re-
sume the glory He had before the incarnation (John 17:5).
Moreover, God freely bestowed on Christ "the name which is
above every other name." Some take "the name" to refer to dignity
or glory, others take it to refer to a particular name such as Lord
or Son of God. But it seems best to conclude that the name Jesus
is meant here; at least such is the inference to be drawn from
verse 11. That was the name given Him after His birth, and it
was given prophetically because He should save His people from
their sins (Matt. 1:21). And the ascended Lord gave that as His
name to Saul of Tarsus on the Damascus Road (Acts 9:5).

"In the name of Jesus" (v. 10) is the way in which every
prayer is to be offered and every knee is to bow. Whether the
word "things" is to be considered as applying to things or intelli-
gent beings is debated. Some argue for a neuter rendering (as in
KJV) and apply the verse to the entire creation collectively as
coming to pay homage to Christ. Others render the areas of
sovereignty with the masculine (as in NASB) and refer those in
heaven to angelic beings, those in earth to living men, and those
under the earth to the dead. It should be noted that "every knee"
does not imply that angels have bodies, nor is there any time element implied as to when complete fulfillment of the prediction
will occur.

Furthermore, verse 11 should not be construed as teaching
that all ultimately will be saved. It simply indicates that at some
future time, in the consummation of all things when Christ judges
the world, all will recognize His lordship. For those who die without putting their trust in Christ as Savior there will be no further
chance. "Now is the day of salvation" (2 Cor. 6:2). As is Paul's
custom, at the end of verse 11 he rises from the Son to the

Father. The ultimate purpose of the exaltation of Christ is to bring glory to the Father. And the immediate significance of the exaltation of Christ is to remind the Philippians of His right to lordship in the church and in their individual lives. Such lordship would bring an abrupt end to all expressions of disunity in the church.

B. PRODUCT: APPLICATION OF THE MIND OF CHRIST (2:12-16).

If the Philippians are to think as Christ thought (v. 5), that mind set will have significant effects in their midst. We now look at Paul's exhortation to apply Christ's example to their church situation. "Wherefore," just as Christ was characterized by a spirit of obedience, so should you be. But to temper any appearance of harshness, he inserts "my beloved-ones," a special mark of tenderness in Philippians (see 4:1, where he uses the term twice). He appeals to their mutual affection for each other as a further ground for their obedience to his exhortations, rather than the authority of his apostleship.

The authority of apostleship looms in the background, however, for obedience whether He is present or absent implies authority to command. Obedience to the gospel and to Paul's apostolic directives had "always" characterized the Philippian church, so Paul is asking nothing new but merely a continuation of the way they have acted all along. "Now much more in my absence," indicates that the absence of the teacher and his inability to deal with their problems on the spot requires even more diligent obedience to the gospel and his exhortations in order to solve the pressing problems in their midst.

Having exhorted to obedience, Paul now issues the command: "Work out your salvation with fear and trembling." Since salvation from sin is a gift of God, as is clearly indicated throughout the New Testament, Paul is not teaching here that one who has received an initial infusion of grace is now to make his salvation complete by self-effort. Nor does it seem that what Paul is talking about is growth toward Christian maturity or sanctification. In this vein, commentators frequently call this an exhortation to "work out" what God in grace has "worked in."

Rather, in this context, Paul appears to be urging his hearers to work out their deliverance or solution to their problems as a congregation. Such solutions will bring about an end to the disease of strife and restoration of the spiritual health of the community. Salvation (sōtēria) may be construed as involving the safety or physical well being of individuals or groups, as is clear from such passages as Philippians 1:19 and Acts 27:34 (where sōtēria is rendered "health" in the KJV and "preservation" in the NASB). "With fear and trembling" indicates a spirit of human inadequacy and the necessity of leaning on divine power and wisdom to solve problems.

Such dependence will prevent problem-solving from being merely self-effort and will guarantee effective results, for God "is at work in you" (v. 13, NASB). The comparison of Philippians 2:13 with Ephesians 2:2 is exciting. According to the latter Satan works in or ,energizes unbelievers; according to the former God moves effectively upon unbelievers. "In you" may refer to in your hearts or inner being but probably here should be rendered "in your midst." God is at work in believers to help them to desire or want (to provide the determination) and to energize or enable them (to provide the strength) to accomplish that which seems good in His sight or to exercise "goodwill." The latter is preferable here because the next verse introduces an exhortation to put away those things that will destroy goodwill among the Philippian believers.

"Do all things without murmurings and disputings" (v. 14, KJV), exhorts the Philippians to a plane of life possible only when God energizes believers, providing the strength of purpose and the strength of performance necessary to live a life of goodwill. "All" stands first in the sentence in the Greek text and emphasizes the all-inclusive nature of the command. The verb "do" is in the present tense, indicating in the Greek continuing action: "keep on doing." Because the Old Testament has much to say about the murmuring of the Israelites in the wilderness against God, some commentators rather instinctively conclude that Paul also is talking about the same kind of sin here. But this almost certainly is not the case. In every other place where this term is used in the New Testament the murmuring or grumbling is against men. Moreover, the whole issue here in Philippians is that certain sins in the church at Philippi prevented true unity. Furthermore, until now there has been no hint of murmuring against God at Philippi. On the whole their faith has been quite exemplary. Murmurings against other believers arise from selfishness and run counter to the example of Jesus described above. "Disputings" may refer only to disagreements or dissensions, but beyond the informal reference it also may have a technical legal sense of litigation and may imply that some of the Philippian believers actually had gone into the law courts with their squabbles, as at Corinth (1 Cor. 6:1-11).

The goal or purpose of these prohibitions of verse 14 is the elimination of all things that would mar their testimony in the community or would destroy their effectiveness as a witnessing community. "That ye may be" is more literally "that ye may become," indicating a state or condition that the Philippians have not attained but might gradually attain. "Blameless" and "harmless" refer respectively to outward and inward conditions. Outwardly their conduct will be above reproach. Inwardly their condition will be literally unmixed or unadulterated or pure. The word used here was employed during New Testament times to describe wine or metals unmixed with impurities. Thus, in their hearts or inward disposition or intrinsic character they would be guileless or uncontaminated. As "children of God," hence members of God's family, living in a community of believers on earth (the Church) they are to be "above reproach" (literally "without blemish," see Col. 1:22), untarnished both in reputation and inner condition. "Above reproach" refers back comprehensively to "blameless" and "harmless."

"In the midst of a crooked and perverse generation" (NASB) indicates the context of this people living above reproach. "In the midst" speaks of the fact that they are to be in the world but not of it, living in the world (with its perverted ethical and religious orientation) but not dominated or characterized by the spirit or mind set of the world (John 16:14, 16). The people among whom they were living were crooked and perverted. They were crooked as opposed to straight, i.e., unbelieving and indocile (Luke 3:5; 9:41). They were perverted, i.e., warped, distorted, twisted in their inner nature or of abnormal moral condition. The term was used especially of limbs misshapen or mutilated or dislocated on the rack. Would it be in order to suggest that such were mutilated on the rack of sin? Beet describes these enemies of the gospel well: "Instead of being upright, they were crooked in character and conduct: instead of being a normal growth, they were deformed cripples. Among such men and in conspicuous contrast to them, Paul desired his readers to be without blemish, thus revealing their divine lineage: *children of God, spotless . . .*" (p. 77).

Among such people the Philippians would certainly "appear as lights in the world." Lights or luminaries or light givers is the same word as in Genesis 1:14, 16 in the Greek translation of the Old Testament (Septuagint). By contrast with the darkness of the unbelieving world and in the midst of it they will appear as the moon and stars, giving forth light. And as the spiritual darkness intensifies in our own day believers will appear to shine ever brighter by comparison. They will, that is, if they are not conformed to this twisted world or pressed into its mold (Rom. 12:2).

As these believers shine in the darkness, they will hold forth the word of life (v. 16). Their light will be a guide to the truth. And to change the metaphor slightly, they will (as the verb often is used) hold out food and drink to others, distributing the bread of eternal life. The verb means not only "hold forth" but also "hold fast," and of course it is necessary to hold fast to the truth if one is to hold it forth.

Then Paul's great pastoral heart is laid bare. If the Philippians are faithful Paul will have occasion to rejoice at the day of Christ, at His judgment seat, when all the work of believers will be tried. Paul is thinking much of that day in this epistle; he already has referred to it in 1:6, 10. At that time he does not want the experience of either the runner or the laborer who has expended all his efforts in vain. And of course if his efforts prove to be in vain on that great day, so will be the efforts of the Philippians; thus here is an implied reminder to them to be diligent in view of the great day when the Lord of all the universe shall preside on the judge's stand and distribute the rewards (1 Cor. 9:24).

C. EXAMPLES: THOSE WHO POSSESS THE MIND OF CHRIST (2:17-30).

1. *Paul* (2:17, 18). Paul suddenly shifts his line of thought in verse 17. He turns from a discussion of the impact of the mind of Christ upon the church at large to examples of individuals who possess the mind of Christ. He focuses on Timothy and Epaphroditus, but in the process says some things about his own situation and outlook that incidentally also classify him as one who possesses the mind of Christ.

"If I be offered" (KJV) appears in the present tense and is a technical term for wine poured over or beside sacrifices. The NASB, "If I am being poured out as a drink-offering," gives the proper sense. The possibility of Paul's martyrdom (the pouring out of his life blood) is clearly evident in his own mind, in spite of the fact that optimism characterizes other verses in the epistle (1:24-26; 2:24). If his life were to be poured out upon, or probably better, beside or in addition to the faith or works springing from the faith of the Philippians, Paul would rejoice. The sacrifice is that of the Philippians who as priests engaging in their priestly duties offer their faith to God. Possibly this offering of sacrifice alludes to their monetary gifts, which were for them a a real sacrifice, and which helped to make possible the furtherance of the gospel. Alongside their sacrifice Paul's lifeblood was the accompanying libation. If Paul is to be martyred, he will rejoice —probably in part because being with Christ would be gain (1:21) and in part because at so great cost he had been permitted to lead his readers to faith. Moreover, he would share their joy or rejoice with them over their faith in Christ.

While Paul evidently did not intend to hold himself up in this passage as an example of one who had the mind of Christ, his complete self-abnegation and concern for them beautifully illustrates Christ's own attitude in the first verses of the chapter. "For the same reason," or better, "in the same way," is an invitation to the Philippians to share his joy. "Rejoice with" is an expression of united experience which not only underscores the close ties between the apostle and the Philippians but also requires close fellowship and thus unity among the believers in Philippi. "With" here is a preposition which in Greek even more clearly than in English involves united experience. If they are to rejoice together with him in the fullest experience of Christian unity, the mind of Christ must be their common possession.

2. *Timothy* (2:19-24). "But I hope in the Lord Jesus to send Timothy to you shortly, so that I also may be encouraged when I learn of your condition" (NASB). "But I hope." In contrast to the thought of being martyred (v. 17) he hopes his situation will improve sufficiently so that soon he will be able to send Timothy to them. "In the Lord" indicates that his plans are governed by the Lord's will, and Paul is not certain about them at the moment.

The purpose of Timothy's visit is that "I also may be of good comfort" (KJV). The fact that he would consider sending faithful Timothy shows something of the importance Paul attaches to communication with the Philippians. Of course he wanted to thank them for their gift to him, but that is not even hinted at here. He wanted rather to comfort them by a good report of his condition, and he sought comfort by a word from Timothy about them — evidently to the effect that the factionalism existing among them had ceased.

"I have no man likeminded" (KJV) does not mean that Paul is comparing Timothy with himself but rather is comparing Timothy with all others. There is no one else who comes close to having such a concern for the Philippians. "Naturally" is literally "by birth-relation" and comes to mean "truly" or "genuinely." Since Timothy had been involved with Paul in founding the church at Philippi or bringing these spiritual children into the world, it is natural that he should have a fatherly concern for them. "Care" is the same word in the Greek here as in Philippians 4:6. Here intense concern for the welfare of others is held up as commendable; there intense concern or anxious care for one's own interest is prohibited.

It is hard to know exactly how to interpret verse 21. On the face of it he is saying of course that no one else he might have sent to them really had the mind of Christ to the degree Timothy did, for they sought their own interests rather than those of Christ. If he had sent away all his other most trusted helpers to run important errands (e.g., deliver Ephesians, Philemon, Colossians, etc.), then it is possible he has no one else on whom he could really count for the moment. The fact that Epaphroditus had risked his life to do some important task for Paul during an especially sensitive period of the apostle's imprisonment (v. 30), implies that he indeed may have been bereft of dependable people who might be at his disposal.* If this is the case, Paul's sending Timothy would show how important this mission was — it might leave him virtually alone.

Martin observes, however, that this may not be an indictment of all Paul's associates but a parenthetical comment on the state of the world around him: "It says nothing about his fellow-Christians; but is rather his solemn reflection when he remembers that, in a world of selfishness and self seeking (cf. Mt. vi. 32), it is such a rare thing to find a man like Timothy who is really anxious to promote the welfare of other people, and to give him-

*Certainly he couldn't send members of Caesar's household or military personnel. Paul could not have included Epaphroditus among the self-seekers but it would have been difficult to send one of the Philippians to deal with the problems in his home church; it would be better to send a trusted representative of the apostle to do that.

self to a fatiguing journey and to the resolving of personal quarrels in the Philippian church" (p. 125).

"You know of his proven worth" (v. 22, NASB). They had known Timothy at Philippi and he had proved himself among them; he had stood the test. "As a son with the father, he has served with me in the furtherance of the gospel." Paul begins as if he were going to write "He has served me as a child serves a father," but changes his statement to recognize the fact that both he and Timothy were bondslaves of Jesus Christ (1:1), who Himself came to take the form of a slave (Phil. 2:7). By inference we might say that Paul and Timothy are in this way linked in exemplifying the mind of Christ. Timothy's concern, like Paul's, was for the furtherance of the gospel — for its spread and triumph.

Evidently Paul sent his letter to the Philippians in the hands of Epaphroditus with the plan of sending Timothy as soon as it became clear how his case would fare in the courts (v. 23). His optimism about an early acquittal led him even to announce plans for coming to Philippi in person (v. 24). But he covered himself with "in the Lord," which is equivalent to saying, "if the Lord wills."

3. *Epaphroditus* (2:25-30). In our world of topsy-turvy values, an insignificant person may have his name splashed across the pages of history for committing a terrible crime but almost never for doing acts of kindness. One of these rare exceptions is Epaphroditus, member of the church at Philippi and friend of Paul. Millions of people all over the world have read about this little-known Christian in the early church and have honored him for his sterling qualities. His only claim to fame is that he showed kindness to the apostle Paul and was concerned for others in his local church. In short, he was one of those uncommon individuals who has possessed the mind of Christ. Sent by the Christian community at Philippi with their gift to Paul, Epaphroditus had served the apostle so diligently that he had worn himself out and had contracted a nearly fatal illness. Now recovered, he returns home with Paul's blessing.

Mentioned only here in the New Testament, Epaphroditus is not otherwise known. He is not to be confused with Epaphras of Colossians 1:7; 4:12. Paul calls him "my brother and fellow-worker and fellow-soldier" (NASB). Lightfoot observes, "The three words are arranged in an ascending scale; common sympathy, common work, common danger and toil and suffering" (p. 123).

"Brother" of course indicates a fellow-believer in Christ. "Fellow-worker" applies to partnership in the work of the gospel and may allude both to their association earlier in Philippi and now in Rome. "Fellow-soldier" refers to joint conflict in Christian warfare. Though Paul uses many metaphors to describe one's Christian service, one of his most graphic is warfare. He is fully aware that the believer's struggle is primarily against spiritual foes — against Satan and all his henchmen (Eph. 6:12). To fight battles with such enemies one cannot use carnal or fleshly weapons (that is, one's own energy and wisdom, 2 Cor. 10:3, 4) but he must have divine weapons and armor (see Eph. 6:11-17).

"Messenger" is in the Greek *apostolos* — one entrusted with a mission. It is too much to claim, as some do, that Epaphroditus was an apostle bringing a gift that was some sort of gospel (good news) to Paul. He was simply their delegate or authorized representative. "Minister" or "servant" is in Greek *leitourgos,* of which "liturgy" is a rough English equivalent. The word was used commonly in New Testament times in a ceremonial sense of work done for religious purposes (Deissmann, pp. 137, 138). So here Epaphroditus' ministry to Paul may be viewed as a sacrifice or oblation, a "liturgy" to God. By extension or application, there is no reason why our daily work should not be viewed as a sacrifice to God. If it is, it will be rendered with a far different spirit of enthusiasm than is usually the case. And of course it cannot be done in a mediocre fashion. A new standard of excellence will characterize work done for the glory of God.

Epaphroditus was so sacrificial in serving Paul that he had become run down and contracted a serious disease or had had a physical breakdown. Word of this had reached Philippi and had caused much concern there. When Epaphroditus heard that his trouble had caused trouble to others, he was very disturbed. "Longed after you all" (v. 26, KJV) is the same construction in the original as in Philippians 1:8, where it refers to Paul's great desire to see the Philippians. "Full of heaviness" (KJV) is the term used to describe Christ's agony in Gethsemane (Matt. 26:37; Mark 14:33). These are strong terms that show the degree of distress Epaphroditus was suffering at the time — not over his own troubles but over the Philippians. In part he may have thought their anxiety would be dispelled by seeing him in good health. Some have suggested that he was a leader in the Philippian church and was overwhelmed with concern for the flock from which he was separated and therefore longed to return to Philippi. The great anguish of Epaphroditus was apparently the reason why Paul "thought it necessary" to return the apostle of good will to Greece. Intimations, especially in the Greek text of Philippians 2:25 and 28, indicate that the originial plan was for Epaphroditus to stay on indefinitely to serve Paul after he had delivered the gift.

In verse 27 Paul vouches for the nearly fatal character of Epaphroditus' illness. "God had mercy on him" implies the hopelessness of the situation from man's point of view and the sovereign power of God over illness. Paul viewed the mercy as extended to himself also because he acutely felt the helplessness of the situation. As a prisoner he was not free to move' around and even attend to the personal needs of Epaphroditus. Moreover, as a brother in the Lord he empathized with the suffering of the sick one. Furthermore, he was disturbed over the great distress that the death of Epaphroditus would cause in Philippi. Beet comments, "Thus one act was, in different ways, kindness to two men equally helpless. Paul's gratitude also teaches that they who share the sorrows of others have in others' joy a special joy of their own" (p. 86). "Sorrow upon sorrow" may refer simply to the general difficulties that Paul had to endure in connection with his imprisonment or possibly to the fact that he was going through some especially trying difficulty, as some have suggested.

In verse 28 Paul returns to his immediate plan to return Epaphroditus to Philippi. "The more carefully" (KJV) is better rendered as in the NASB "the more eagerly." Paul sent him the more eagerly because of his own rejoicing over Epaphroditus' recovery and the patient's concern over conditions in Philippi. And upon seeing the restored one you "may recover your cheerfulness" (literally), which had been marred by word of his critical illness.

Verse 29 seems to provide further indication that the original plan had been for Epaphroditus to remain with Paul indefinitely. Now Paul has to assure the Philippians that their messenger was not a deserter or somehow was incapable of rendering the service they wanted to provide for Paul. Possibly also there was some other cause for alienation about which we know nothing. At any rate, Paul found it necessary to send a word urging the Philippians to receive him in the right spirit. That would have been unnecessary if he was merely returning after delivering a gift. The apostle encourages the Philippians to receive Epaphroditus "with all gladness," with a joy that harbors no suspicions of his motives or condemnation of his actions. "Hold men like him in high regard" (NASB), for reasons given in verse 30.

The Greek of verse 30 is somewhat difficult and readings vary slightly in different manuscripts, but the general meaning is clear. For the cause of Christ or the gospel Epaphroditus had been at the point of death, risking or hazarding his life to supply the Philippians' "lack of service" toward Paul. The last part of the verse is not a rebuke on the part of Paul that the Philippians had neglected him but is simply a statement that he was there to do what they' could not do for him because they were hundreds of miles away. "Service" is the same word *leitourgos* used in verse 25.

In commenting on Paul's commendation of Epaphroditus in verse 30 Martin observes, "Such a word brings its own challenge and rebuke to an easygoing Christianity which makes no stern demands, and calls for no limits of self-denying, self-effacing sacrifice. Here is a man who gave little thought to personal comfort and safety in order to discharge his responsibility" (p. 134). Of course we must "hold men like him in high regard" (v. 29), for they are among the few who manifest the mind of Christ.

FOR FURTHER STUDY

1. Read the sections on Timothy and Epaphroditus in E. E. Hiebert's *Personalities Around Paul* for further discussion of these individuals.

2. How will the fruit of the Spirit as listed in Galatians 5:22, 23 promote unity in a church fellowship?

3. How do you square true humility with a proper appreciation of one's gifts?

4. Can you think of other persons in Paul's list of associates who also might have been included in Philippians 2 as individuals possessing the mind of Christ? What about Luke or Titus?

5. Try to develop more fully Paul as an example of one who possessed the mind of Christ, using the Book of Acts and other epistles. Bible dictionaries or Bible encyclopedias also might be helpful.

CHAPTER 6

The Biographical Appeal for Unity: Answers From Paul's Experience to the Problems Causing Disunity

(Phil. 3:1-21)

Two special problems have arisen to threaten the unity of the Philippian church. Whether they have made considerable inroads among the believers or are merely a hazard to them is not clear. At any rate, Paul feels called upon to deal with Judaizers and perfectionists. The former argued the necessity of circumcision and law keeping for salvation. The latter insisted on the possibility of arriving at a stage of sinless perfection in this life. Such teachings would upset the believers at Philippi and would cause factional disputes among them. Paul naturally felt obliged to move against these dangerous views. He could have countered with a theological discourse but chooses rather to respond largely on the basis of personal experience. All the righteousness he had gained through law keeping was totally inadequate and he gave it all up for the superior righteousness which came on the basis of faith in Christ. Now that he was in Christ and possessed His righteousness, he had not reached a state of sinless perfection. Christian perfection was not absolute but progressive in this life.

A. PAUL'S RIGHTEOUSNESS (3:1-16).

1. *Not of the Law but Christ* (3:1-11). "Finally" (*to loipon*) sometimes is used in Paul's letters to introduce his conclusion, and the Greek may mean "finally" or "in conclusion." But it should not be assumed here that Paul was about to "sign off" and then suddenly had another thought that kept him going for two more chapters. Certainly he would not have concluded without the thank you in 4:10 and following and should have written that before coming to "finally." It also may be argued that when Paul began such a short epistle he had fully in mind all the topics he intended to take up. Furthermore, by the time Paul wrote, this Greek expression no longer had such a specific meaning. It may signify a variety of things, such as "furthermore," or

"henceforth," or as Beck translates, "Now, then." We are not merely multiplying words on an insignificant point. Paul must not be accused of being like the modern preacher with poor organization and poor terminal facilities who "concludes" several times before coming to an end. If we have a high view of inspiration, neither Paul nor any other writer of Scripture has the option of personal afterthoughts to be thrown in at the whim of the moment.

"In the Lord" indicates the true sphere of joy, in contrast to confidence in the flesh or carnal joy. As one is in Christ and faithful to Him, His joy flows in and through the believer. This is the great teaching of abiding in Christ as presented in John 15. Moreover, one should rejoice both because he is the Lord's and because of what the Lord has done for him.

"I do not hesitate to write the same things to you" is difficult to understand. Some suggest that it refers to repetition of "rejoice"; such a repetition would be a safeguard against despondency under trial. Others hold that it is an allusion to warnings against dissensions within the fellowship. Several think it refers to exhortations in other Pauline letters now lost. Yet others apply it to warnings against false teachers that he made in person while with them and is now about to reiterate.

Warning against Judaizers. After voicing his concern for the Philippians, Paul's tone suddenly changes: "Be on the lookout for the dogs; be on the lookout for the evil workers; be on the lookout for the self-mutilators." Three times the apostle thunders away in the imperative mood. The implication is that these false judaizing teachers have not yet invaded but might appear on the horizon at any time. Any reception of them would nullify the true gospel and introduce a major cause for disunity among the brethren. They must rally to a man around the standard of justification by faith alone.

"Dogs" clearly refers to the Judaizers. Jews had considered Gentiles as dogs (see, for instance, Matt. 15:26); now the tables are turned. Jewish Christians who misrepresent the gospel are described as dogs. These were individuals who insisted that the kingdom could be entered only through the gates of Judaism — through circumcision and law-keeping. They refused to accept the decision of the Council of Jerusalem (Acts 15) that absolved Gentiles from keeping the law and they violently opposed Paul, the great apostle of the Gentiles and of Christian liberty, at every opportunity. The full significance of the term "dog" is lost on a modern American or European who is used to well-groomed and well-fed house dogs. In the ancient Near East they were animals of the street, ferocious and despised beasts belonging to no one and annoying the people of a town with their incessant barking and howling during the night. In this context they may be thought of as yelping constantly at Paul and annoying him as he tried to serve God.

These who preach the necessity of good works to obtain salvation are described as "evil workers" (cf. 2 Cor. 11:13). The word translated "concision" in the King James Version is used only here in the New Testament and is a play on the term for "circumcision." The word means "mutilation" and describes the Judaizers as circumcised individuals without proper faith in and obedience to God and therefore enjoying nothing more than physical mutilation. The physical act of circumcision accomplished nothing for them.

Characterization of the true circumcision. In contrast to the dogs, alias evil workers, alias self-mutilators, Paul says, "We" (emphatic) "are the [true] circumcision" (v. 3). We are the ones who have the true covenant relation with God as partakers of the New Covenant (remember that circumcision was the sign under the Old Covenant that one belonged to God). We are the ones who possess the circumcision or purification of the heart (cf. Jer. 9:25, 26); the circumcision of the Judaizers is merely outward — in the flesh. The reason why Paul could say "we are the circumcision" is threefold.

(1) "Who worship by the Spirit of God" is the reading of the better Greek manuscripts. The verb rendered *worship* here is used of ritual service as in Hebrews 8:5; 9:5; 10:2; 13:10 and of worship or service generally as in Luke 1:74; Romans 1:9. It is applied especially to service rendered to God by Israelites as His chosen people (Acts 26:7). Vincent observes, "A Jew would be scandalised by the application of the term to Christian service" (*Commentary,* p. 93). The fact that the same word may apply to one's worship and service should help to remind the modern believer that all our service, whether it be work done at employment, service in the home, studying at school, or something else, is in a sense an act of worship and ought to be done well for the glory of God (1 Cor. 10:31). The fact that worship is "by the

Spirit of God" underscores the fact that believers serve under the direction of the Holy Spirit and by His enablement.

(2) "Who boast in Christ Jesus" is a favorite expression of Paul's; it appears more than thirty times in his epistles. The believer exalts Christ and His finished work as the means of establishing favor with God rather than any good works on his part.

(3) "Who put no confidence in the flesh" looks especially to the Judaizers' tendency to depend heavily on circumcision, Jewish descent, and legal observances, and hence extends to all external privileges. But the reference must be expanded to include all aspects of the human nature without divine enablement. Vincent well observes, "It properly characterizes, therefore, not merely the lower forms of sensual gratification but all — the highest developments of life estranged from God, whether physical, intellectual, or aesthetic" (*Commentary,* p. 94).

Paul's false confidence. In dealing with the Judaizing error, Paul now turns more specifically to his own experience of placing confidence in the flesh. For the moment he puts himself on the same ground as his opponents, showing that by their standards, in his unconverted state he had greater ground for confidence in the flesh than they ("I have more," v. 4). He takes this approach to make clear both to the Judaizers and the Philippians that he knows what he is talking about. He speaks from valid experience as an authentic, full-blooded Jew. He once had all that his opponents had and far more, but he renounced all that for the superior way in Christ.

In verses 5 and 6 he lists seven advantages which could give him a reason for glorying in the flesh. The first four are hereditary and the last three his by personal choice or effort. "Circumcised the eighth day." Paul begins at the point on which the Judaizers were most vociferous: circumcision. He was not circumcised in adult life at the time of conversion as proselytes were, nor at the age of thirty as Ishmaelites were, but on the eighth day after birth as any true Hebrew child under the law ought to be. "Of the stock of Israel." His parents were not grafted into the covenant people (proselytes) nor Idumeans or Ishmaelites, but were descended from Israel, the prince of God. "Of the tribe of Benjamin." Though a very small tribe, Benjamin had much to commend it. Its progenitor was the only one of the twelve patriarchs born in the land of promise. It gave Israel its first king and Paul

(Saul) bore the name of that ruler. Jerusalem and the temple lay within its boundaries. The tribe remained loyal to the house of David after the division of the monarchy. "A Hebrew from Hebrews" means a Hebrew from Hebrew parents, who, although living outside Palestine in the dispersion (Tarsus), maintained Jewish language and customs and manner of life; he was no Hellenist. In the nomenclature of the day, a Jew merely traced his descent from Jacob; a Hebrew did also but additionally had to speak Hebrew (Aramaic) and retain Hebrew customs.

Paul now turns to his three advantages that came as a result of personal commitment. "As to the law, a Pharisee." He was a member of the strictest and most law-abiding sect of Judaism. The Pharisees were the most orthodox defenders and expounders of the law and were revered as such by all Jews. Beet observes, "This principle, viz. that the favour of God is to be obtained by obedience to authoritative prescriptions of conduct, found in the Pharisees its strictest exponents and adherents. And Paul was a *Pharisee*" (p. 93).

"As to zeal, persecuting the church." Paul was not only a member of the sect of Pharisees in good standing, but he had such zeal for the law and the maintenance of Judaism that he mounted a personal campaign against the church. Not only did he seek to destroy Christians in Jerusalem (Acts 8:3) but in other places as well. In fact, he was on a persecuting mission to Damascus when the Lord met him and he was converted (Acts 9:1-19; 23:3ff.; 26:9-12). As is clear from the references in Acts 22 and 26 just noted and the passage here in Philippians, Paul carried the memory of his opposition to Christians vividly throughout his ministry and up to his arrest in Jerusalem and imprisonment in Rome. In fact, he still was smitten with the enormity of it when he wrote to Timothy near the end of his life. But he took comfort in the fact that God forgave him because he did it "ignorantly in unbelief" (1 Tim. 1:12, 13). "Church" is the translation of a Greek word meaning "called out ones" and in the New Testament commonly refers to the community of all who are called by and to Christ and who confess Him as Lord. Sometimes it alludes to particular congregations of believers gathered in specific places (e.g., Rom. 16:5; 1 Cor. 1:2; Philem. 2).

"As to righteousness which is in the law, blameless" (see Acts 3:1). Reference here is only to Paul's own estimate of his outward actions in his unconverted state or the evaluation that others of his Pharisaical company might place on his actions. As Müller well summarizes, "Conduct and manner of life, ceremonial and moral relation to the law, left nothing to be desired" (p. 111). Paul no longer felt that he was blameless in those days of zeal for the law or that he was justified by keeping the law, as is clear from such statements as Romans 2:3 and Galatians 2:16.

Paul's renunciation of Jewish boasting. In verse 7 Paul solemnly renounces his Jewish boasting. "The things which [the sort of things or classification to which belong the things just noted] were gains to me [were a source of enrichment] I have counted [as an act of deliberate judgment] loss for Christ." "Counted" is in the perfect tense in Greek, indicating an action in the past that continues to have effect in the present. Presumably this major decision on the part of Paul took place in the Damascus Road encounter or shortly thereafter as Paul rearranged his spiritual furniture and completely revolutionized his goals and standard of values. The comparative uselessness of his previously held system of work-righteousness appears in the word "loss," which in the papyri (Greek literature written on papyrus sheets in Egypt about the time of the New Testament) is used to refer to bones thrown out on the street to dogs. Actually these things were a hindrance to gaining righteousness in Christ. Pharisaic righteousness endangered the soul's salvation. For the sake of Christ and in order to gain Christ's righteousness, which comes entirely on the basis of faith, one must renounce all other systems by which he builds up his own merit with God.

The Greek particles at the beginning of verse 8 vigorously introduce an expansion of the apostle's confession in verse 7. It is hard to translate the original; perhaps the New International Version rendering is as good as any: "what is more." Now Paul turns to the present tense, "I continue to count." And the "all things" here is a considerable advance on the "things" of verse 7. There he renounced things of a sort that a faithful Jew might boast of. Now "all things" refers literally to anything that might be considered as meritorious works by the natural man and serves as a complete indictment of all religious effort. The apostle reaches a new height of exaltation: "I continue to count all things but loss in view of the surpassing worth of the knowledge of Christ my Lord." This experiential knowledge of Christ eclipses all else by comparison. Rainy has beautifully observed, "Christ had come into the life of Paul as a wonderful knowledge. Becoming thus known to him, He had transformed the world in which Paul lived, and had made him conscious of a new order of existence, so that old things passed away and all became new" (p. 153).

"For whom I have suffered the loss of all things" refers to a specific time in the past ("suffered" is in the aorist tense), undoubtedly Paul's conversion, when he suffered the confiscation, was literally "mulcted," of all things. Vincent aptly comments, "In that great crisis all his legal possessions were lost" (*Commentary*, p. 101). Paul did not mind because he had come to recognize that justification was by faith in the finished work of Christ, not the works of the law. Therefore he can say, "I count them refuse, that I may gain Christ." "Refuse" may be either excrement or garbage thrown from the table to the dogs. To "gain Christ" is to appropriate Him, to win His justifying righteousness, and to enjoy all the grace and glory that attaches to Him.

Gaining Christ and possessing His righteousness. Paul now elaborates on what is involved in gaining Christ. "Found in him" is passive and bears the thought of discovered or proved to be. Apparently here it concerns recognition by others that Paul is truly united to Christ. Some would apply this to a future day of judgment but verses 9 and 10 seem to apply to this life, with verse 11 looking toward the future. To be in Christ is to be linked to Him in living relationship so His life pulsates throughout our beings, so His orientation to the experiences of life becomes ours, so His power and motivation spur us on. This concept is further elaborated in Galatians 2:20, the figure of the vine and the branches in John 15 and in Paul's Mars Hill speech where he says, "For in him we live, and move, and have our being" (Acts 17:28).

If Paul is in Christ, joined to Him in a new spiritual relationship, then he possesses Christ's righteousness, for in the salvation experience the righteousness of Christ is put to the account of the believer and truly becomes his. That, simply phrased, is what is involved in the great doctrine of imputation, stated in Romans 4 and elsewhere. If Paul is in Christ, possessing His righteousness, then his own righteousness — any resulting from his own effort in careful observance of prescriptions of the law — is null and void, is totally superfluous, totally useless ("not having a righteousness of my own, even that which is of the law"). Man does not come to God on his own terms and on the basis of his own efforts, but on God's exclusive terms — through Jesus Christ: "I am *the* way" (John 14:6). God will not have man reminding Him of human

effort and successes; "all our righteousnesses are as filthy rags" in
his sight (Isa. 64:6). Righteousness comes through the channel
of faith — "through faith in Christ." Righteousness is received
on the condition of faith — "by faith" — that is, by means of
utter dependence on and belief in God's provision through the
work of Christ on the cross ("faith in Christ"). "Where is boasting then? It is exalted. By what law? of works? Nay: but by the
law of faith" (Rom. 3:27).

Knowing Christ more fully. "That I may know him" (v. 10) is
an infinitive of design or purpose in the Greek. It is necessary to
go back to verse 8 to get the drift of Paul's thought. "I continue
to count all things but loss . . . that I may gain Christ and be
found in him, in order that I may know him." Paul already enjoys
a certain level of experiential knowledge of Christ (v. 8), which
must have been considerable indeed if we remember that he is now
in prison near the end of a long and fruitful ministry which involved
the writing of several New Testament epistles. But apparently he
considers present knowledge paltry judged by future possibilities.
We continue to learn more of those with whom we are most
intimately associated. To know Christ more fully would be to
know to a greater degree "the power of his resurrection." Paul has
spoken elsewhere of this power which raised Christ from the dead
(Rom. 1:4; 2 Cor. 13:4). That kind of divine power could do
anything. Paul had seen it raise him from the jaws of death at
Lystra (Acts 14:19, 20), had called upon it to raise from the
dead a lad named Eutychus at Troas (Acts 20:9-12), and had
seen and felt it operative on a host of other occasions. Yet he
longed for an even greater demonstration of that power in the
future.

Knowing Christ more fully would also involve "the fellowship
of his sufferings," partnership with Christ in His sufferings that
others might be brought to faith in Christ. Beet aptly notes, "They
who for Christ's sake, and in order to save men, endure hardship, are sharing His sufferings for the world's salvation. For their
sufferings, like His, are caused by man's sin, are endured in loyalty
to God and love to mankind, and are working out God's purpose
of mercy" (pp. 96, 97). It is remarkable that Paul should utter
this desire to know the fellowship of Christ's sufferings after all
he had gone through. A man who years earlier could list the catalog of persecution detailed in 2 Corinthians 11:23-28 and who had
at the time of writing spent four years in prison (two in Caesarea

and two in Rome) for the sake of the gospel, apparently did not need to make such a request — yet such was the totality of his dedication to Christ.

The totality of that dedication is further exemplified in "being conformed to his death." This does not necessarily mean that he wants to suffer martyrdom for the cause of Christ but probably looks more to passages such as Romans 8:29; Philippians 3:21; and Galatians 2:20. To be "conformed to" is to be "pressed into the mold of"; and to be pressed into the mold of the whole thought pattern related to the death of Christ would involve death to the old life and the operating principle of sin as presented in Romans 6. This kind of perfection Paul deals with in Philippians 3:12-16.

In verse 11 he looks longingly toward that complete conformity to Christ that will come at the time of the resurrection and presence with Christ. This is not the resurrection *of the* dead, but resurrection *from among* the dead. In other words, it is not a general resurrection of the dead but a resurrection of believers from among the whole group of the dead as is pictured in such passages as 1 Corinthians 15. At the time of this resurrection, believers will be truly conformed to Christ in that they will have a new glorious body like His. "If by any means" is not really an expression of uncertainty of the outcome but is more an indication of the determination of Paul "by any means," "at any cost," to be faithful to the cause of Christ.

2. *Not Yet at Stage of Perfection* (3:12-16). In these verses Paul makes it clear that he does not claim to have reached a state of perfection in faith and grace, which evidently would come only at the resurrection. He seems to intimate in verses 15 and 16 that there is some divergence of opinion on this point of perfectionism which needs to be dealt with. Otherwise it will be a real or potential source of disunity.

"Not that I have already attained" counters any thought of actual attainment. The verb has no object but probably refers to all that is included in verses 8-11. Two verbs with different tenses appear in the original. "Have obtained" or received is in the aorist and refers to a simple act in the past (the time of conversion); "am made perfect" is in the perfect tense and refers to the process of life up to and including the present. Paul is saying in effect, "Neither at salvation nor up to the present have I been perfected." "But I continue to pursue," to strain every nerve; growth in grace is progressive and is achieved only with considerable effort. Phillips translates the last half of the verse, "But I keep going on, grasping ever more firmly that purpose for which Christ Jesus grasped me." In no uncertain terms Christ grasped or laid hold on (seized) Paul on the Damascus Road, bringing him to a conversion experience. From that moment on it seemed clear to Paul that Christ had an important purpose for him in terms of his spiritual development, beyond the special mission he was to fulfill as apostle to the Gentiles. Paul for his part would pursue with utmost diligence attainment of this goal of spiritual perfection that Christ had set before him.

In verse 13 Paul starts with a direct appeal ("Brethren") and then places "I" and "myself" in an emphatic position in the original; "I do not count myself yet to have grasped." Whatever others may say, I am still a learner; I have not arrived. Kennedy asks, "Why such strong personal emphasis? Is it not a clear hint that there were people at Philippi who prided themselves on having grasped the prize of the Christian calling already? Paul has been tacitly leading up to this" (p. 458).

"One thing" is left hanging in the Greek without a verb; evidently "I do" may be supplied properly. "Forgetting those things that are behind" may refer either to Paul's successes in Judaism or in the Christian life. In either case forgetting cannot mean blotting out the memory of something, because he has rehearsed his position in Judaism above and his activities for Christ elsewhere. Forgetting means rather that he will not allow the past to influence his present attitude or conduct. Remembering the past in Judaism might only encourage a tendency to put confidence in the flesh and would only hinder his progress. Remembering his successes in his Christian career might lead to self-satisfaction and relaxation of effort. Coupled with the negative of forgetting is the positive "stretching forward to the things which are before." Vincent observes that this is "a graphic word from the arena. The body of the racer is bent forward, his hand is outstretched towards the goal, and his eye is fastened upon it" (*Commentary,* p. 110), "The things which are before" apparently refers to the events of the last day: resurrection, judgment, rewards.

Verse 14 continues the figure of the runner straining every nerve and muscle as he runs the race. "I press on toward the mark," says Paul. "Mark" is the translation of a Greek word which indicates that on which one fixes his gaze; it is used only here in the New Testament. In classical Greek it was commonly a mark for shooting at. Perhaps it is valid here to think of it as the end of the course already in view to the runner. The prize is not otherwise identified but is apparently the everlasting heavenly glory. "The high calling of God in Christ Jesus" seems to apply to the fact that God's call came to him to enter the race and obtain the prize. The "high" or "upward calling of God" was the call to conversion which Paul heard on the Damascus Road and which is addressed to all who come to believe today. The calling is "of God" because He is the author and "in Christ Jesus" because He is the person of the Godhead in whom the call is issued.

Today the Lord Jesus continues to issue the divine invitation, "Behold, I stand at the door, and knock: if any man hear my voice, and open the door, I will come in to him, and will sup with him, and he with me" (Rev. 3:20). The message of Philippians 3:14 clearly means that merely answering the call to salvation is not enough. One is expected to run the race of life to the glory of God with all the energy he can muster.

Having shown from his own experience that Christian perfection is not attainable in this life, Paul now proceeds to call for unity of conviction on this point in the Philippian church (vv. 15, 16). Surprisingly, he addresses those who are "perfect." The English translation is correct; the Greek word is the same as in verse 12. He evidently is not speaking in irony; there is no hint of that in the context. How then can he consider some to be perfect (and he includes himself among them — "us") when he has just declared categorically the impossibility of perfection? The answer is found in the use of perfection elsewhere in the New Testament. Look, for instance at Ephesians 4:12-16; Colossians 1:28; 4:12. In those passages a person is considered to be perfect who has reached a certain degree of spiritual stability and maturity — no longer a child tossed about with every wind of doctrine. Evidently, then, perfection may be thought of as relative and absolute. In this life believers never will reach absolute perfection (v. 12) but all believers are exhorted to achieve a certain stage of spiritual maturity which is necessary for the effective functioning of the church (v. 15; Eph. 4:12-16, etc.).

"Of this mind" refers to agreement with Paul on the proposition set forth in the previous verses: Christian perfection is progressive and there is a need to press on toward ultimate perfection with all diligence. Apparently there were some at Philippi who were "otherwise minded." Martin comments, "The use of the verb *phronein* shows that it was more than an intellectual difference; it betrayed a different outlook and affected the conduct of those whom Paul has in mind. Clearly there were some who were teaching that it was possible to be 'perfect' in a final sense here and now" (p. 155). Paul's approach to such is that truly mature Christians will know better and that he is so sure of his position he believes "God shall reveal even this to you." To "reveal" is to lift the veil and impart light from heaven. Paul's approach is correct and proper here. No amount of cajoling by apostles, bishops of evangelicalism, or church councils will persuade people of the truth. True persuasion comes from God through the agency of the teaching ministry of the Holy Spirit: "He will guide you into all truth" (John 16:13).

Verse 16 is difficult to translate and harder yet to interpret. To begin with, "let us mind the same thing" is not in the best manuscripts and should be omitted. Vincent interprets the verse to mean, "Whatever real Christian and moral attainment you may have made, let that serve as a rule for your further advance" (Vincent, *Word Studies,* p. 451). In that spirit Beck translates, "Only be guided by what we have learned so far." Beet renders the verse, "Only whereto we have attained, let us walk by the same" (p. 89), and argues that Paul is here exposing the danger of turning aside from the path in which the Philippians obtained spiritual life and in which they have made considerable progress. Real progress will be along the lines already made (p. 105). Martin observes, "This verse, which reads literally, 'Only as far as we have attained, by the same let us walk,' is a tacit and tactful way of calling the readers to an acceptance of the truth as Paul has expounded it earlier in the chapter" (p. 156). Kennedy translates, "Only, so far as we have come, let us keep to the same path" (p. 460). And in a similar vein Müller observes, "Notwithstanding all difference of opinion which there may be [in Philippi] . . . the present duty is to walk in the light of that unto which believers have already come. We have to move forward in the same line, one of mind, true to what we have already attained" (p. 127). Whatever else we say, this verse has to be interpreted as a call to agreement with Paul, to being steady on the high road of faith and Christian growth, and to unity of the brethren. It is interesting to note that the verb translated "walk" means to stand in a row or walk in a line in an orderly fashion. It would describe a body of people going somewhere together.

B. PAUL'S EXAMPLE (3:17-21).

An example to follow. Paul has been opposing Judaizers and perfectionists, both of whom would seek to follow absolutes — the former the law and the latter a certain ultimate Christian standard. If Paul removes both patterns, he should substitute another. He now offers himself as a living example to believers. No sooner has he set forth his own example, however, than he feels obligated to steer them away from the example set by certain enemies of the gospel. Then he goes on to speak more at length of the walk of the true believer.

Again he addresses the Philippians as "brethren," showing his intimate spiritual attachment to and unity and equality with them. Then he commands them, "be unitedly imitators of me." The construction (found only here in the New Testament) does not say that they are to be followers of Christ together with him but that they are to join together in imitating him. Here is another of the many expressions of unity or unified action in the book. The injunction would seem to be pure egotism if we did not put it in a larger context.

For instance, in 1 Corinthians 11:1 he told the church at Corinth: "Be ye followers of me, even as I also am of Christ." In other words, they were to follow or imitate him only as he evidently was following Christ. It was only as Christ was in evidence in his life that Paul could command others to follow his example. But of course the Philippians may not have had the Corinthian letter by this time. There is plenty in Philippians 3, however, to make clear what he is trying to say. Presumably he was not asking them to follow his actions so much as his teachings just noted — of which he was the embodiment. For instance, his example included a renunciation of all man-made righteousness, a commitment to the position that perfection was not attainable in this life, and a determination to pursue with all his energies the higher plane of Christian living. Moreover, he urges in the latter half of verse 17, "observe those who walk according to the pattern you have in us." "Us" would certainly include Timothy and Epaphroditus (see chap. 2 and 1 Thess. 1:6; 2 Thess. 3:7, 9) and possibly others whom they knew. In other words, there were other like-minded individuals who would serve along with Paul as an example for them.

An example to avoid. Paul turns his attention next to an example not to be followed (vv. 18, 19). Who the "many" are has caused considerable debate. Some have felt they were heathen, but this must not be the case. The whole context deals with problems and problem people within the church. Earlier expositors considered them to be Judaizers; most recent commentators believe they were libertines who interpreted Christian liberty as freedom from all moral restraint. If the latter is true, Paul is faced with three errors in this chapter: the Judaizers, the perfectionists, and the libertarians. Interestingly, these "walk about" ("walking in circles" may not be too extreme a translation) instead of walking in line or walking in step, as did followers of the apostle (v. 17). Paul had repeatedly warned the Philippians about such persons, probably on visits during his third missionary journey, and possibly even in written warnings. "Weeping" occurred not only because of the injury to the church by these professing Christians but also because of the peril to their own souls. "Enemies of the cross of Christ" are not necessarily those who opposed the cross as such but the whole ideology of Christianity to which the death of Christ on the cross was central. In any case, their enmity is more clearly spelled out in verse 19.

The enemies of the cross are described in a fourfold way. (1) "Whose destiny is perdition." If they were Judaizers, their adherence to the law as a means of salvation cut them off from the effects of Christ's death on Calvary as the only means of redemption. If libertines, they were simply bereft of any real understanding of the centrality of the cross to the message of Christianity. (2) "Whose god is their belly [appetites]" may describe dissolute persons whose supreme concern was the belly or Judaizers who sought to force observance of all kinds of laws relating to food and drink. (3) "Whose glory is in their shame" could apply to sensualists who were addicted to all sorts of disgraceful lusts or to Judaizers who gloried in circumcision (shame made equal to private parts or the circumcised member, cf. Gal. 6:13: "glory in your flesh"). (4) "Who set their mind on earthly things" reveals the ultimate source of the perversion noted above. A life ordered according to worldly measures and standards bypasses or repudiates the cross of Christ and righteousness which comes by faith in the accomplishment of the cross and is therefore destined to perdition.

Walk of the believer. After his parenthesis about enemies of the cross, Paul now returns to talk more at length about the walk of the true believer. "Our" is put in the emphatic position in Greek in contrast to "those who set their mind on earthly things." "Our citizenship" or "commonwealth" is in heaven. The fatherland of the believer with all its rights and privileges is in heaven, and his conduct of life should be in accordance with that citizenship. He should "seek those things which are above, where Christ sitteth on the right hand of God" (Col. 3:1). This mention of another commonwealth with its privileged citizenship would have a special appeal for the Philippians, who lived in a Roman colony and possessed the coveted Roman citizenship with all its rights and privileges. Such individuals have a double allegiance, but primarily they are citizens of heaven and thus are resident aliens in a foreign country. "We wait for" is a strong word that indicates an earnest, patient waiting and expectation of Christ's return, when He will bring full deliverance from all sins and infirmities and complete the process of progressive perfection on which Paul spoke earlier in the chapter. Viewing the Lord Jesus Christ as "savior" put Him in direct contrast or conflict with Caesar, for since the days of Augustus Caesar it had been common to revere the emperor as divine savior (at least in many of the provinces). As Savior, Jesus Christ will bring deliverance from the trials of a hostile and alien world.

The believer's expectation. In verse 21 one of the major accompaniments of His coming is described: He "shall fashion anew the body of our humiliation." To "fashion anew" is to give our bodies an altered shape and guise, to change the outward and visible vesture in which the human spirit is clothed. The implication is that there is continuity between the present and future bodies. Perhaps the experience of Christ is a help. His glorified body after the resurrection was recognizable, down to the scars in His hands and side. This does not mean, of course, that we shall bear scars in our glorified bodies; in His case they probably remain to remind redeemed humanity in heaven of His work on their behalf. "The body of our humiliation," not a "vile" body, but a body characterized by weakness and finally death, is to be changed. The nature of the change is not detailed but only hinted at in the classic passage on the Resurrection in 1 Corinthians 15:42-44, 49, 51-54. It will no longer be subject to death, will be released from much of the limitation we now endure, and will be a fit vehicle for our regenerated personalities.

"That it may be conformed to the body of his glory" is stronger than "fashion anew" used above and implies some sort of share in the inward constitution of the body of Christ. "When he shall appear, we shall be like him" (1 John 3:2). This process of transformation takes place by "exertion of the power whereby he is able even to subject all things unto himself." Müller observes, "The divine power is always a power at work, an active divine energy which in addition to everything else . . . is also able to subject all things to Himself. His is a sovereign power to which all things are subordinate — all earthly power and authority, enemies and death . . . This power of Christ is the guarantee that He is able to make our body of lowliness like unto His body of glory" (pp. 135, 135). The word used here for power (*energeia*) occurs only in Paul's writings. It is power in exercise and is always used to denote supernatural power. Periodically, as we contemplate evil enthroned in the councils of nations, the weakness of the church, and even personal inability and frustration, it is well to remember that He possesses "the power [working] whereby he is able even to subject all things unto himself." His sovereign hand is still in control, though His immediate purposes may not always be evident.

FOR FURTHER STUDY

1. Using Bible dictionaries and whatever other helps are available to you, study the history of Tarsus and the tribe of Benjamin.

2. How could a Pharisee think he was blameless before the law? Can you find any indications in the Sermon on the Mount (Matt. 5-7) that keeping the law was utterly impossible as Jesus interpreted it?

3. Enlarge on the study of Paul prepared in connection with Philippians 2. There concentration was on Paul as an example of one who had the mind of Christ. In what other ways may he be upheld as an example of the believer?

4. Study 1 Corinthians 15 to see what it has to say about the nature of the glorified or resurrected body.

CHAPTER 7

Exhortations That Will Lead to Unity

(Phil. 4:1-9)

A. Plea for Steadfastness (4:1).

In the first verses of chapter 4 Paul issues a series of exhortations, one of which directly involves a problem of disunity; the rest, if heeded, would certainly promote unity. Steadfastness in the Lord, forbearance toward others, an effective prayer life and a controlled thought life, would all contribute to unity in the Philippian church or any other body of believers.

"Therefore," connects 4:1 with the last verses of chapter 3. Bearing in mind your citizenship in the heavenly kingdom and the hope of a coming Savior, "stand fast in the Lord" — the practical result of such magnificent truths. This verse heaps up terms of affection for the Philippians. Only the Thessalonians enjoyed anything like Paul's affection for the Philippians. They are not only "brethren" (3:1, 17) but "my brethren dearly beloved and longed for." "Longed for" (ardent desire), only here in the Greek New Testament, recalls the longing expressed in 1:8 and is no doubt a result of the unique excellence of the Philippian believers and their love for Paul.

"Joy and crown" fit together, for joy is the emotion expressed by one who has children in the faith, and crown (*stephanos*) was either a festive wreath worn by merrymakers or the garland awarded a victor in an athletic contest (1 Cor. 9:25). It is not the diadem of a prince or priest. As Paul's crown, they would be proof that "he did not run or work in vain" (Phil. 2:16) and at Christ's coming would be the reward for his faithful service. If they are to be involved in Paul's reward at the judgment seat of Christ, they must be the abiding fruit of his efforts. Therefore he encourages them again to "stand fast [firm] in the Lord," to maintain their spiritual position as becomes citizens of the heavenly kingdom, in spite of external attack and internal erosion of false doctrine and dissension. "In the Lord" designates the protected defense bastion in which the believer may stand. As Beet says, "the personality of the Master whom they serve being the only firm standing ground of the Christian life" (p. 108). "Beloved" intensifies this loving appeal.

B. SETTLEMENT OF DIFFERENCES BETWEEN WOMEN IN THE CHURCH (4:2, 3).

Some sort of disagreement had blown up between two prominent women in the Philippian church. "This direct reference to a difference of opinion between two women of prominence in the Philippian Church is probably the best comment we have on the slight dissensions which are here and there hinted at throughout the Epistle" (Kennedy, p. 464). What this dispute was we are only left to guess, but there is no hint it was doctrinal in character. Presumably Euodia and Syntyche had been bickering over some differences of opinion or approach. The argument may even have concerned important issues of how best to present the gospel or to deal with problems of Christian living. The disagreement had by now been of long standing and evidently was public knowledge, otherwise Paul would never have addressed them publicly through a letter to the whole congregation. No doubt Epaphroditus had brought news of the disagreement when he delivered the Philippian gift. Such squabbles will cast a cloud over any congregation and will hinder its usefulness for God. In dealing with the problem Paul does not censure or blame but treats both equally and positively. "I appeal to" (Modern Language Bible) or "urge" (NASB) best reflect the tone of the Greek; these translations are neither too harsh or too tender but carry a gentle firmness. Note that the verb is repeated with each name to put both individuals on an equal footing. And the appeal is to "be of the same mind in the Lord." It would not do simply to urge these women to get together and bury their differences, because no doubt each felt she was right. "Their quarrel would dissolve itself if they brought it into His presence, and as their Master, gave Him His proper place in their relations with each other" (Hiebert, *Personalities,* p. 165). If they would come to the disagreement with the mind of Christ (Phil. 2), the problem could be resolved.

When two individuals are involved in a public disagreement as Euodia and Syntyche were, it is often difficult, if not impossible, for them to bring about a reconciliation on their own. They need the help of a third party. So in verse 3 Paul takes the next necessary step by beseeching Syzygus to step in to help bring the women together. Some of the editors of the Greek text and many commentators feel that the proper name Syzygus should be used here instead of the common noun *syzygus,* which means "yokefellow." The argument some offer is that all other persons in this context are listed by name, and it would be hard to know exactly who was to take the initiative in settling this problem unless he were named. "Help" means "to take hold together with" and indicates the kind of negotiation or arbitration Syzygus was expected to engage in.

Paul next proceeds to commend these women for their brave service in the cause of Christ, along with other members of a hard-working team. This mention would on the one hand point up their value to the cause of Christ and thus smooth the way as reconciliation was attempted, and on the other point up the deplorable results of allowing such squabbles to continue. As Hiebert observes, "The rendering 'labored' does not adequately bring out the force of the original, which implies united action in the face of opposition and strife. The metaphor emerged from the arena, and pictures these women as having served as Paul's fellow soldiers in the battle to establish the gospel at Philippi" (p. 166). Clement is not otherwise known. Other fellow laborers, perhaps unnamed because they had died in the meantime, may have been forgotten on earth, but they are remembered by God and their names are in "the book of life." They are therefore assured of life everlasting and their proper rewards. The concept of a book of life appears both in the Old and New Testaments; see for instance, Exodus 32:32; Daniel 12:1; Luke 10:20; Revelation 3:5; 13:8; 20:12.

C. REJOICING, PRAYER, AND THE RESULTANT PEACE OF GOD (4:4-7).

Rejoicing. In these verses appears a series of exhortations without grammatical links. "Rejoice in the Lord" reminds us of Philippians 3:1, but here there is the addition of "always." That means at all times and in all places. It means to rejoice in the Lord when circumstances are most promising and to rejoice in the Lord when everything is wrong (cf. Hab. 3:17, 18). Happiness and joy are two different emotions. Happiness is apt to be more related to circumstances and to involve a mood of gladness. Joy, at least Christian joy, is more a delight of the mind arising from assurance of a present or future rooted in God regardless of circumstances. It often is closely akin to peace or serenity of conscience. To be sure there is a certain natural joy that may come from a variety of successes, but joy unrelated to circumstances is a fruit of the Spirit (Gal. 5:22). It is not something that can be worked up on one's own.

To the one who today may say to Paul, "But you don't understand my situation," the apostle would answer: "I am not asking something easy. I have been in prison for four years as I write this, and the Philippians face severe trials at the hands of a pagan society." The controlling factor in this exhortation is "in the Lord," for it is faith in Him which makes rejoicing under difficulty a possibility. "The Pauline appeals to joy are never simply encouragements; they throw back the distressed churches on their Lord; they are, above all, appeals to faith" (Martin, p. 167).

Forbearance. "Let your forbearing spirit be known to all men" (v. 5, NASB). This spirit of forbearance or goodwill, fairness, magnanimity, graciousness, is apparently to be directed primarily toward pagan society rather than merely to characterize relationships within the church, for it is to be known "to all men." If exercised within the church, it would, however, go a long way toward eliminating any disunity that might exist. The relationship of this exhortation to rejoicing is clear. If one is upset by circumstances, he will find it difficult to exercise goodwill and graciousness toward others. Conversely, if his joy is in the Lord and he is able to handle more effectively the problems of life, he will find it much easier to be gracious to others. The exhortations to rejoice and demonstrate a spirit of graciousness are tied to the observation that "The Lord is at hand." This could of course mean that the Lord is near and observes all that we do; such a reminder would encourage us to do His will. More likely it means that the return of the Lord is at hand, when He will reward the faithful and vindicate His oppressed people. A similar thought appears in James 5:8: "Be ye also patient; establish your hearts, for the coming of the Lord is at hand."

Cure for anxiety. "Be anxious in nothing." Anxiety here is "not the forethought which enables us to guard against coming troubles, but the useless and painful care which merely brings the sorrows of to-morrow to spoil the pleasures of to-day" (Beet, p. 113). (See also Luke 10:41.) It is biblical to make all possible preparation for the future* but one must live a life of faith, not being consumed with worry over the supply of needs or the handling of difficult situations in life. A classic passage on this subject is Jesus' beautiful statement in Matthew 6:25-34. The English of that teaching does not always bring out the truth of the original; for instance, verse 31 should be translated, "Therefore have no anxiety." "In nothing" (Phil. 4:6) is a prohibition against anxiety of every kind. Beet perceptively concludes, "This anxiety arises from the common delusion that our happiness and well-being depend upon the possession of material good. It injures our body; and, by filling the mind with earthly care, blocks out the elevating influence of heavenly things; and exposes us to the terrible temptation of seeking in forbidden paths relief from present distress" (p. 113).

The cure for anxiety is faith, according to Jesus' teaching in Matthew 6, but faith is implemented or fostered through prayer, and that is the special emphasis of the present passage. "In nothing be anxious; but in everything by prayer"; the totality of inclusion on the agenda of prayer directly counterbalances the totality of exclusion from the agenda for worry. "Nothing is too great for God's power; nothing too small for his fatherly care" (Vincent, *Commentary*, p. 134). "Prayer" comes from a word that emphasizes prayer as an act of worship; it is the general word for prayer and invokes only God. "Supplication" is petitionary prayer, a cry of personal need, earnest request for some special good, and may also be addressed to man. "Thanksgiving" should be a significant element of prayer, in part because appreciation or gratitude should characterize every beneficiary of good and in part because thanks for benefits received or for fulfillment of the promises of God stimulates faith and hope for the present and future. "Let your petitions be made known to God," frame them specifically and present them to God. Don't deal in hazy generalities — "bless all missionaries everywhere." Even though God is omniscient or all-knowing, He has directed that we remind Him of specific needs. Then we shall receive specific answers. We shall be blessed in seeing specific answers to specific prayers and He will be glorified as we count these many blessings and name them one by one.

The peace of God. If one lives in such close fellowship with

*For example, "Go to the ant, thou sluggard" (Prov. 6:6) is another way of saying, "Be industrious in preparing for the future."

God that in faith he turns over all the affairs of life to the heavenly Father, then the fruit of this believing prayer will be the "peace of God." This is not peace *with* God, which is wrought by justification, but the inward peace of the soul, the inward rest that comes from utter dependence on an omnipotent, gracious, and loving Father. Anxiety with its accompanying feeling of helplessness disappears from a life that is totally committed to the all-powerful Sovereign of the universe. This peace "passes all understanding" — of those who come in contact with the believer and even of the believer himself. The Greek signifies that it is an absolutely unique kind of peace transcending every human thought. It is not, therefore, merely greater in degree than that provided by earthly considerations, but is totally different in kind.

"Shall keep" is a promise of divine commitment; it is not a prayer or wish to be translated "May the God of peace keep." "Keep" is a military term and may be translated "garrison about" or "keep watch over" or "stand sentry." Such a concept would have had special meaning to Philippians living in an imperial garrison town. "The peace of God . . . shall garrison about your hearts and your thoughts." Our hearts are the innermost recesses which constitute the seat of feelings, the will, and the thoughts. Thoughts are the products of mental activity. The peace of God "will keep watch over heart and mind so that nothing can cause unrest and discord, because everything is placed trustingly in the hands of God by the prayer of faith" (Müller, p. 143). This peace is available only "in Christ Jesus" who is the refuge and bulwark of our spiritual lives.

D. CONTROLLED THOUGHT LIFE (4:8, 9).

"Finally" probably is not to be interpreted as another attempt to conclude the epistle (see on 3:1) but is better understood or translated "and so" or "in this connection." So, if the peace of God is to be experienced, the believer has to take some steps himself. We already have seen that faith and prayer are necessary concomitants to peace, but there is more. One must be careful what he fills his mind with, what he dwells on, because mental furniture also helps to create the right atmosphere or attitude when the challenges of life crowd in on us. It is of course impossible to decide not to think about something, because in the process of making such a determination one thinks about it all the more. The command here is to "let your mind dwell on" a variety of

noble and positive things, to "reflect upon and then allow these
things to shape your conduct" (Martin, p. 171). Meditation pre-
cedes, then follows action. "Whatsoever," as many things as,
"suggests number and variety in each of the following classes"
(Beet, p. 115). Perhaps Vincent is right in his conclusion that,
"The exhortation is not to the cultivation of distinct virtues as
such, but each virtue represents general righteousness of life
viewed on a particular side . . ." (*Commentary,* p. 137). Whether
one accepts such a conclusion or concentrates on these concepts as
separate virtues, there is helpful instruction in this verse.

"True" or "truthful" things are those which, as opposed to
falsehood and error, correspond in thought, word, and deed to the
norm of moral ideals as revealed in Jesus Christ ("I am *the* truth,"
John 14:6). "Honest" or "honorable" is a translation of a word
that is hard to put into English. It signifies worthy of reverence,
deserving of respect, exhibiting a dignity that grows out of moral
elevation. To Beet, "It suggests the dignity which pertains to conduct worthy of Christ" (p. 115). That which is "just" or "right"
is human conduct that tallies with the divine standard of action
toward God, one's neighbor, and one's self. "Pure," unstained by
evil of any kind, is purity in a moral sense, in motives as well as
acts. "Lovely," only here in the New Testament, is that which
inspires love, or endears one who does such things. Beet describes
it as the "attractive sweetness of Christian excellence" (p. 115).
"Of good report" is that which sounds well when spoken of, praise-
worthy. "Virtue" is a Greco-Roman concept of excellence (moral,
intellectual, physical, material) and "praise" is the verbal recognition of this excellence. Lightfoot suggests the following explanation for the latter part of the verse, as if Paul were eager not to
omit any possible ground of appeal: "Whatever value may reside in
your old heathen conception of virtue, whatever consideration is
due to the praise of men" (p. 162).

It is not, of course, enough for the Philippians to reflect on these
tremendous concepts in verse 8. They must now act. Not only
must the Philippians obey the apostle's precepts, they also must
follow his example. "Those things" or "the things" are taken
generally as referring to the virtues enumerated in the previous
verse. "Learned" is intellectual apprehension; "received" is moral
approval. "Heard" and "saw in me" refer to the example of Paul
in personifying these virtues in their midst. These things they
have come to know and accept and have seen in the apostle as a

living example, they are now to "do" — or more in the spirit of the Greek, "practice" (continuing action).

As noted in 3:17, this is no egotistical command on the apostle's part. He did not claim to have arrived, but he did claim a certain level of Christianity maturity. And what Paul said in a sense has to be said by every Christian leader today. A pastor, teacher, or other Christian worker must be an example to his followers and can hardly expect them to do what he has not done — to arrive at a level of spiritual maturity to which he has not risen. He must be able to say in a sense, "follow my example." Chilling thought, isn't it?

To the obedient comes the promise: "and the God of peace shall be with you." "The Giver of peace *will* ever *be with* those who keep His commands" (Beet, p. 116). "God is 'the God of peace' only to those who are at one with him. God's peace is not sentimental, but moral" (Vincent, *Commentary,* p. 140). Though peace with God is based on reception of Christ's work on our behalf by faith alone, obedience to the commands of God is the condition to enjoying the peace of God and the fullest blessing and sense of the presence of the God of peace. God never leaves the believer (Heb. 13:5), and we do not need to pray for Him to be present in a church service or on other occasions, but the sense of His presence or His fullest blessing is conditioned on our response to His commands.

FOR FURTHER STUDY

1. What does Scripture say about a "book of life"? Study the references given in this chapter and see if you can locate others with the help of a concordance.

2. Make a list of things or situations you have worried about. Try to write beside each some sort of biblical recipe for handling it in the future so you will be "anxious in nothing."

3. Make a list of ways in which you feel you are not an example to others. What can you do to rectify the situation. List Scripture bearing on your shortcomings.

4. Using the exhortations in Philippians and references in other books of the Bible, write your own description of what it means to rejoice in the Lord or to have the joy of the Lord.

CHAPTER 8

Thanksgiving for Their Gift: A Representation of Their United Action

(Phil. 4:10-20)

This section contains the specific occasion for the writing of Philippians: the arrival of a gift from the church there in the hands of Epaphroditus. Kennedy observes, "The very fact of his accepting a present from them showed his confidence in their affection" (p. 469). Because of the criticism leveled against him in various places to the effect that he was making the gospel a means of livelihood (e.g., 1 Thess. 2:5; 1 Cor. 9:3-18; 2 Cor. 11:8, 9), he was careful about taking gifts from the churches and often supported himself by his own labor. Evidently he had no fear of slander in the Philippian church because he received their gifts.

Revival of concern. "I rejoiced" and "in the Lord" continue two themes frequently expressed in this letter: the tone of joy and mutual fellowship in Christ. The gift of the church was prompted by their union with the Master and was received with a like spirit of gratitude. "Greatly" is in the emphatic position in the Greek and calls attention to this occasion for special joy. "Now at last you have revived your concern for me" (NASB). Vincent picturesquely translates, "You caused your thought for me to sprout and bloom afresh, like a tree putting out fresh shoots after the winter" (*Commentary,* p. 142). Though "now at last" or "now at length" suggests delay and even a chiding for delay, there is no harshness in the Greek here; and the last half of the verse makes it clear that Paul has no criticism of them. "Wherein," in the matter of my welfare, "you were all along taking thought," shows that the interest was there. "But you were lacking opportunity" all the while you were taking thought. It is not clear what prevented them from sending their gift, but presumably it was lack of means for transmitting it.

Parenthesis on contentment. Lest there be any misinterpretation of what he has just said, Paul hastens to declare that his joy is not just satisfaction over relief of personal needs (v. 11). "Not that I speak according to want"; it is not the joy of a starving man. Then appears a parenthetical discussion of contentment in verses 11b-13. Martin perceptively observes, "This is not a fatalism or indolent acquiescence which cuts the nerve of ambition or smothers endeavour. . . . It is, on the contrary, a detachment from anxious concern about the outward features of his life. This, in turn, arises from his concentration upon the really important things . . . above all, upon the closeness of his fellowship with Christ on whose strength he constantly draws" (p. 175). "I have learned" views his whole learning experience up to the present. "In the state in which I am" refers to the condition in which Paul found himself at the moment. Though "whatsoever" is not in the original, presumably the apostle would be able to say the same thing about the other experiences connected with his ministry. One might draw such conclusions if Paul could sing in the inner cell of the Philippian jail at midnight with his back bruised and bleeding.

"Content" means literally "self-sufficient." It was a favorite word with the Stoics who believed that a person should be sufficient unto himself for all things. Of course Paul's conviction was not that he was self-sufficient but that his sufficiency was in Christ irrespective of circumstances. Beet puts it well, "Christian contentment is not a narrowing down of our desires to our poor possessions, but a consciousness of infinite wealth in Christ, in whose hands are all things already working for His servants moment by moment their highest good. He who has this consciousness is independent of his environment" (p. 119).

"I know," as a result of having learned in the school of life, "how to be abased" or brought low. The same word is used here as in Philippians 2:8, where Christ humbled Himself; it carries the thought of voluntary acceptance of a lowly position. "And I know how to abound" (KJV), how to be abundantly furnished, how to prosper and yet retain the spirit of humility. It probably requires more effort to learn how to be prosperous and not be puffed up by it than to be debased and not crushed by it. "In any and all circumstances I have learned the secret" is about the best possible translation of the middle of the verse. "To be full" is used elsewhere of feeding animals or multitudes of human beings (as in the case of Christ's miracles in the Gospels); "to be hungry" is the opposite of full. "To abound" is the same as "to be full"; "to suffer need" refers to one in serious financial difficulty or in debt. "All things" (in the emphatic position), not "all these things" as some read, includes not only the things mentioned in the previous verse but all other things as well. "I can do" — Paul here makes an assertion of virtual omnipotence. There have to be conditions, of course, for man is not God. Perhaps we should say he can do whatever lies within the line of duty and necessity. Or perhaps we should say with Beet, "In Christ Paul is morally omnipotent" (p. 121). This immediately introduces the source of Paul's strength: Christ. Though Christ is not named in the best manuscripts, clearly the reference is to Him. "In him who strengthens me" may better be translated "in him who infuses strength into me." From the inward union with Christ is derived the strength to do all things Paul has to do.

Partners in affliction. Just as in verse 11 Paul wanted to guard against the thought that his joy rose merely from satisfaction over relief of personal needs, now (v. 14) he wants to guard against any thought that he lightly esteems their gift. "Nevertheless," do not think that just because I am content with all circumstances, I make light of your gift. "You did nobly in that you became partners in my affliction." They shared with him his hardship at Rome and helped to relieve it by their contribution. They did a noble thing, a beautiful thing, and probably the most beautiful part of it all was not the money gift and the blessing it brought but the sense of their sympathy and companionship. The root of the word translated "became partners in" is *koinōnia,* now so familiar in the vocabulary of the church.

Past generosity. In verse 15 the apostle calls the Philippians to witness concerning their past generosity to him. "Now you also know, Philippians" — the unusual address of his readers by name gives definiteness and earnestness to his statement. "In the beginning of the gospel" certainly applies to the beginning of the preaching of the gospel in Europe — in the province of Macedonia about ten years earlier. "When I went out from Macedonia" could refer to a gift the Philippians presented him just as he left Macedonia (Acts 17:14) after ministry at Thessalonica and Berea. Or, more likely, it alludes to the gift Paul received from Macedonia while he was in Corinth, not long after leaving the northern province (2 Cor. 11:9). "No church entered into partnership with me for an account of giving and receiving, but you only."

The terminology here is from the business world of the day. The giving was all on their part in this case; the receiving all on his part. Although a few commentators try to make out a case for Paul's providing spiritual gifts in return for monetary gifts, this concept is missing entirely from the context, and disturbs the teaching here. The most that can be said is that they are joining with him in the spread of the gospel in a spiritual partnership. He is providing the labor of preaching; they are providing financial support. But he does not minister to them in return; he is engaged in missionary effort elsewhere. "You only" — no one else joined in at the time and no one else immediately followed their example.

But these remarkable Philippians had sent him financial support even before he left Macedonia. It is to be remembered that Paul's three main preaching stops in Macedonia were Philippi, Thessalonica, and Berea, in that order. Thessalonica was some eighty-five miles southwest of Philippi. How long the apostolic company preached there is uncertain. According to Acts 17:2 Paul taught in the synagogue for three sabbath days (requiring a lapse of three weeks); apparently the Jews became too hostile thereafter and he spent his time with the Gentiles. Certainly Paul did not remain there more than three or four months. Yet even during that short time the Philippians sent him two gifts ("once and again") to help meet his needs.

Present rewards. "Not that" (v. 17) introduces a corrective to verses 15, 16. Paul wants to make it clear that he does not desire gifts primarily for his own benefit. In verse 11 he used the same construction as a corrective to the idea that his joy over the gift rose from his deep sense of want. He says, "Not that I am seeking" as a habitual attitude "the gift," whatever gift they may make from time to time; but "I am seeking," repeated for emphasis of a different view, "fruit," spiritual fruit which their generosity yields to themselves — the reward of their liberality. As they continue to give, this reward is "increasing" or "abounding" to their "account" or "credit." Some commentators view this as a piling up of reward to be dispensed at the judgment seat of Christ, and that is certainly true; but it should not be restricted to that. Acts of Christian kindness and the faithful conduct of ministry enrich and develop the person who performs such acts; in some degree rewards are immediate. Are we not, as Christian workers, sometimes just as thankful for what the performing of some act of kindness did for the development of the character and personality of a friend as we are to be the recipient of that act? That is what Paul is talking about here.

Supply for the apostle. In verse 18 Paul returns more specifically to the benefits of the Philippian gift to him personally. "I have received in full," used in the papyri as a technical expression employed in a business receipt, "and abound" indicates that not only are his needs met but their generosity has been so great he has much more than enough. "I am amply supplied" (NASB) is not a climax to the first two verbs but introduces what follows: "having received from Epaphroditus what you sent." The gifts they sent are now described as "an odor of sweet smell," an expression frequently appearing in the Old Testament to describe a sacrifice acceptable to God (e.g., Gen. 8:21; Lev. 1:9, 13, 17); a "sacrifice acceptable, well pleasing to God." "The gift to Paul obtains a greater worth and a higher significance when seen as an offering brought to God. What was given towards Paul's needs was sacrificed to God Himself. For, indeed, what is done to one of the least of His brethren, is done to the Lord Himself (Matt. 25:40)" (Müller, p. 151).

Supply for the Philippians. The mention of sacrifice in verse 18 raises the possibility that the gifts of the Philippians may have been very sacrificial on this occasion; they certainly were at an earlier time (2 Cor. 8:2ff.). In fact the "but" (Greek) which introduces verse 19 indicates some impoverishment. The Philippians were God's instruments in abundantly meeting all Paul's needs. Now apparently they have great need of their own. By inspiration comes the promise, "My God shall amply supply all your needs." It is interesting to observe that the same word for supply is used here as in verse 18 to describe Philippian supply for Paul; and the word used for "need" here is the same as used for Paul's need in verse 16. "My God," the God whom I know by personal experience to be really concerned about His own and faithful in meeting their needs, will supply "all your needs" — material and spiritual. The measure of the supply is infinite: "*according* to his riches." The manner of the supply is "glorious," in such a fashion that His glory will be manifested. The means or source of the supply is "in Christ Jesus." In Him dwells all richness (e.g., Col. 1:27; 2:3) and in union with Him we are linked to the source and supply of limitless divine wealth.

As Paul thinks about God's goodness to His people and their supply for him in his need, a doxology wells up within him

(v. 20). "To God, even our Father," to God who is the Father of Paul, the Philippians and all other believers through faith in Christ and who graciously cares for them, "be the glory," the majestic perfections that call forth praise and adoration, "unto the ages of the ages" — an endless succession of indefinite periods, forever. "Amen" is a closing expression of confirmation, the owning of something as valid and true.

FOR FURTHER STUDY

1. What can you learn from Bible dictionaries or other Bible study books about Paul's trade and when he used it to support himself?

2. Look up in a concordance to see what Paul has to say about "sufficient" or "sufficiency."

3. Look up articles on "rewards," "crowns," and "judgment seat of Christ" in Bible dictionaries and other Bible study books to see what the New Testament teaches about rewards for the believer.

CHAPTER 9

Conclusion:
Greetings From All to All

(Phil. 4:21-23)

A. GREETINGS (4:21, 22).

As is customary in his other letters, Paul concludes Philippians with greetings and a benediction. He is careful as he sends final greetings to include the whole Christian community, just as he has been throughout the letter. "Salute" or "greet every saint in Christ Jesus." This is the only time in the New Testament that "saint" appears in the singular; in all other fifty-seven times it is plural and even here it is prefaced with "every." There is no place in the New Testament where one saint (patron or otherwise) is elevated above the others. A saint is a holy one, set aside for God's purposes. New Testament saints are "in Christ Jesus," for only as one is related to Christ by faith can he be called a saint. And everyone so related is a saint; so all true Christians are saints.

According to his usual practice, Paul does not name individual believers in his Philippian greeting. Whatever his reasons for not doing so, in this way he avoided jealousy or hurt feelings. Names are prominent, however, in letters to the churches at Rome and Colosse, where the apostle had not been at the time of writing and with which he evidently was trying to establish some rapport. If he wanted to send personal greetings he could do so via Epaphroditus. Who was to do the greeting is not specified, evidently the elders or other leaders of the church who read the letter to the congregation. "The brothers that are with me salute you," creates something of a problem of identification. In 2:20 he had not been very satisfied with the degree of dedication of some of the Christian workers, but now apparently includes them in his salutation anyway. Of course Timothy and Epaphroditus would be among the group.

In verse 22 the greeting is broadened to include "all the saints" at Rome as sending greetings. But those "of Caesar's household" are singled out. Members of Nero's family are not implied here but rather various servants, slaves, and functionaries of the

Emperor's household. Though naturally members of the palace staff were included, others in the service of the Emperor elsewhere could be also. The fact that these people are mentioned here shows that at the very nerve center of the Empire in the official circles there were now believers as a result of Paul's imprisonment.* Their mention also would have a certain appeal to the Philippians who as Roman citizens would "sit up and take notice," so to speak, on learning that the gospel had penetrated the imperial government.

B. BENEDICTION (4:23).

The concluding benediction is typically Pauline. "The grace of our Lord Jesus Christ be with your spirit." Grace as unmerited favor is the basis on which salvation and all subsequent spiritual and material blessings come. Grace is communicated for Christ's sake, and is possible because of His substitutionary death on the cross. "With your spirit" is the preferred reading in the better Greek manuscripts. Müller concludes, "The Apostle prays that the grace of Christ be with their 'spirit,' by which man's whole life is governed and which is so very much dependent on God for guidance" (p. 155). Only as His spirit of humility (chap. 2) works with our spirits can we develop attitudes that will enable us to get along with one another better. Only as the grace of our Lord Jesus Christ remolds our entire orientation to life does it make possible the unity of believers, which is, after all, the great theme of Philippians.

FOR FURTHER STUDY

1. Make a comparative study of the conclusions of Paul's epistles. How are the benedictions similar or different?

2. Read Philippians in one sitting in a version you have not read before. What new truths impressed you during the reading?

---

* It is amazing to note that the gospel had spread from the hillsides of Palestine to the palace of Caesar in less than thirty years.

Bibliography

Alford, Henry, *The Greek Testament*. With revisions by Everett F. Harrison (Chicago: Moody Press, 1958).

Beet, Joseph A., *A Commentary on St. Paul's Epistles to the Ephesians, Philippians, Colossians, and to Philemon* (London: Hodder and Stoughton, 1890).

Deissmann, G. Adolf, *Bible Studies* (Edinburgh: T. & T. Clark, 1903).

Duncan, George S., *St. Paul's Ephesian Ministry* (New York: Charles Scribner's Sons, 1930).

Ellicott, Charles John, *A Critical and Grammatical Commentary on St. Paul's Epistles to the Philippians, Colossians, and Philemon* (Andover: Draper, 1876).

Harrison, Everett F., *Introduction to the New Testament* (Grand Rapids: Wm. B. Eerdmans Publishing Company, 1971).

Harrison, Norman B., *His in Joyous Experience* (Chicago: Bible Institute Colportage Assn., 1926).

Hendriksen, W., *A Commentary on the Epistle to the Philippians* (Baker, 1962).

Hiebert, D. Edmond, *Personalities Around Paul* (Chicago: Moody Press, 1973).

Hunter, A. M., *The Letter of Paul to the Philippians* (Richmond: John Knox Press, 1959).

Jamieson, Robert; Fausset, Andrew R.; and Brown, David, *A Commentary, Critical Experimental, and Practical, on the Old and New Testaments*. Reprint Edition (Grand Rapids: Wm. B. Eerdmans Publishing Company, 1945).

Kennedy, H. A. A., "The Epistle to the Philippians" in *The Expositor's Greek Testament*. Reprint Edition (Grand Rapids: Wm. B. Eerdmans Publishing Company, n.d.).

Lenski, R. C. H., *The Interpretation of St. Paul's Epistles to the Galatians, to the Ephesians, and to the Philippians* (Columbus: Lutheran Book Concern, 1937).

Lightfoot, J. B., *Saint Paul's Epistle to the Philippians* (London: Macmillan and Co., 1888).

Martin, Ralph P., *The Epistle of Paul to the Philippians* (Grand Rapids: Wm. B. Eerdmans Publishing Company, 1959).

Meyer, F. B., *The Epistle to the Philippians* (London: Religious Tract Society, 1905).

Moule, H. C. G., *The Epistle of Paul the Apostle to the Philippians* (Cambridge: Cambridge University Press, 1934).

Mounce, Robert H., "The Epistle to the Philippians," in *The Wycliffe Bible Commentary* (Chicago: Moody Press, 1962).

Moyter, J. A., *Philippian Studies: The Richness of Christ* (Downers Grove, Ill.: Inter-Varsity Press, 1966).

Müller, J. C., *The Epistles of Paul to the Philippians and to Philemon* (Grand Rapids: Wm. B. Eerdmans Publishing Company, 1955).

Plummer, A., *A Commentary on St. Paul's Epistle to the Philippians* (London: R. Scott, 1919).

Rainy, Robert, "The Epistle to the Philippians," in *The Expositor's Bible*. Reprint Edition (Grand Rapids: Wm. B. Eerdmans Publishing Company, 1943).

Robertson, A. T., *Paul's Joy in Christ* (Nashville: Broadman Press, n.d.).

Strauss, Lehman, *Devotional Studies in Philippians* (New York: Loizeaux Brothers, 1959).

Tenney, Merrill C., *Philippians: The Gospel at Work* (Grand Rapids: Wm. B. Eerdmans Publishing Co., 1956).

Vincent, Marvin R., *The Epistles to the Philippians and to Philemon* (New York: Charles Scribner's Sons, 1906).

Vincent, Marvin R., *Word Studies in the New Testament*. Reprint Edition (Grand Rapids: Wm. B. Eerdmans Publishing Co., 1946).

Walvoord, John F., *Philippians: Triumph in Christ* (Chicago: Moody Press, 1971).

Wuest, Kenneth S., *Philippians in the Greek New Testament* (Grand Rapids: Wm. B. Eerdmans Publishing Co., 1945).

Listed below are those Bible translations specifically referred to in this study.

The Holy Bible. The Authorized Version or King James Version. Referred to in this study as KJV.

Beck, William F., *The New Testament in the Language of Today* (St. Louis: Concordia Publishing House, 1964).

The Holy Bible: The Berkeley Version in Modern English (Grand Rapids: Zondervan Publishing House, 1959).

New American Standard Bible (La Habra, California: The Lockman Foundation, 1960). Referred to in this study as NASB.

New International Version (New York: New York Bible Society, 1973).

Phillips, J. B., *The New Testament in Modern English* (New York: The Macmillan Company, 1962).

Williams, Charles B., *The New Testament: A Private Translation in the Language of the People* (Chicago: Moody Press, 1949).